Unwavering PATHS

Unwavering PATHS

FAITH-FUELED STEPS TO FLOURISH AS A SINGLE MOMMA

MELISSA A. BROWN

About *Acacia of Hope*

Thank you for your purchase of this book.

A portion of sales goes to helping mothers and their children
in Africa through Acacia of Hope. Acacia of Hope's mission
is to empower the people of Africa spiritually, educationally,
and economically. It provides opportunities to those who
deserve it the most while sharing God's love.
You can learn more about our mission at
www.acaciaofhope.org.

Psalm 121:1-8

A song of ascents.
I lift up my eyes to the mountains—
where does my help come from?
My help comes from the Lord,
the Maker of heaven and earth.

He will not let your foot slip—
he who watches over you will not slumber;
indeed, he who watches over Israel
will neither slumber nor sleep.

The Lord watches over you—
the Lord is your shade at your right hand;
the sun will not harm you by day,
nor the moon by night.

The Lord will keep you from all harm—
he will watch over your life;
the Lord will watch over your coming
and going both now and forevermore.

Dedication

This Psalm was written as a song, sung by weary travelers, reminding us to place our trust in God throughout every step of the journey. I dedicate this book first to my Lord and Savior, my Everlasting Father and my Song.

I also dedicate it to you, dear momma. My prayer is that this book blesses you, encourages you, and strengthens you as you walk the path of single motherhood. May you always remember the strength within you during the hard days, and find deep peace in the beautiful ones. May your eyes and heart continually look up to the One who loves you beyond measure.

Contents

Introduction   xi

Chapter 1: Meeting Jesus in the Morning   1

Chapter 2: Peace at Home   13

Chapter 3: Organized Chaos   25

Chapter 4: Purposeful Planning   37

Chapter 5: Master the Hustle   49

Chapter 6: Fueling Your Passions   60

Chapter 7: Parenting with Intention   73

Chapter 8: The Other Parent   87

Chapter 9: To Date or Not to Date   99

Chapter 10: Cultivating Community   113

Chapter 11: Mending the Soul   125

Chapter 12: Meeting Jesus at Midnight   137

Conclusion   149

Notes

Introduction

Do you ever wonder why it feels like you continually fall short despite knowing you have done all you can? You know, somehow it feels like no matter how hard you try throughout the day, you feel like you have completely failed your children and yourself. You got him to soccer practice on time, but you forgot his water bottle. You helped her complete the homework, but it did not make it to the bookbag. Your fridge is full of food, but nothing you have made seems to satisfy your tween child.

The after-dinner walk to burn off a few calories just cannot happen; your body is exhausted. The new devotional, which you purchased over three months ago, still lies unopened by your bed; your eyes are tired. The birdcage needs to be cleaned. The dishes need done. The laundry moved over to the dryer, but you are on empty. You have given your complete all today, and yet, you feel you have fallen short. Whether you are a single momma by choice or by circumstances beyond your control, the everyday difficulty of motherhood can be so grueling.

Carrying the daily responsibilities of both a mother and a father can be overwhelming most days. There are a number of days when it takes the very last ounce of your energy just to get the kids settled into their beds at night, allowing you only a moment of solitude to shed tears before bed. Quiet tears of a difficult workday, tears of not being enough, tears of hard. It is in those quiet moments that the weight of it all can feel particularly heavy, and it is easy to question your success as a momma on your own.

I have spent numerous days feeling like a mom-failure. It was not for lack of doing my ultimate best.

It was because I lacked stepping stones that went somewhere.

I was very good at hopping to any stone I could jump onto because, in the moment, I just needed to survive. What I did not realize was that these stones were taking me nowhere in the long term; I was just surviving survival mode. Before I knew it, I looked back and wondered how time had passed, but yet I felt that time had not moved at all. My child was older. I was older. But I did not feel that I had progressed beyond just getting through the day. I deserved more.

And so do you.

Staying where you are—enduring, wandering, pondering, barely living—will only keep you where you are. The goal of a *single parent* is not just to survive, although many times it can feel like that. The goal of a *Christian momma* (notice the word changes) is to raise our children to be soldiers of Christ in confidence. Though it is difficult to stay on this path when you are juggling so much on your own, it is possible.

Our goal is to navigate the hardships of single motherhood by unearthing practical stepping stones that will lead to long-term prosperity for us and our children. Amid the exhaustion and hardships, we want to be confident in where we are and that our future is bright. Rather than barely holding it together on the daily, each day, we desire to feel the success of being a faith-filled momma on our own, instilling values and creating a loving home, even if at times it feels like we are barely holding it together.

No matter if you are fluttering through life moment by moment, or even second by second, unsure of where you will land, know that you have everything within you to reach your goal of being a successful single mother, confident in both your present and your future. Together, we will navigate these windy paths, moving from chaotic aimlessness to confident progress that leads to toward a trail of long-term success.

Momma, you got this.

Jesus Mornings

Chapter One

JESUS IN THE MORNING

Beep. Beep. Beep. Beep. Beep.

Flailing your arms around, you attempt to grasp your excessively loud alarm clock with both eyes shut. You literally roll yourself out of your full-size bed and force yourself to find your grounding as you make your way to the bathroom.

The steamy shower wakes you insufficiently, but the brewing hot espresso will be an improvement. Your foggy brain has already made a mental list of all that needs to be done for the day and the pertinent issues you must deal with at hand. Somehow you will manage making two dozen chunky chocolate chip cookies for your youngest son's classroom party for tomorrow even though you have to work late tonight. Your preteen daughter thinks slamming doors in your face while stating that she wants a new family is acceptable; a conversation needs to happen. That sweet little baby of yours has hit the milestone of crawling, and your house is not as babyproof as you thought.

From the shower, the sound of your lastborn son's little feet alerts you. "Goodness . . . he is already up. I haven't even made breakfast yet." Shaving your legs is no longer an option at this point. Perhaps tomorrow. Somehow, insanity must happen over the next forty-five minutes in order to get all the children clothed, fed, and "happily" on the almost-missed bus.

The madness of the morning sets up your day. Hysteria spills into your day job—you are never really able to catch up on any of your professional work—and lands heavily in the evening as the laundry appears now to look like the Leaning Tower of Pisa. Even your crisp carbonated soda did not seem to provide a pep in your afternoon step. Though you made it through another day, your mind never settled, let alone your heart. The idea of repeating yet another day not only disheartens you but makes you feel that your excitement for life is diminishing. In moments like these, when the chaos feels all-consuming, it's easy to lose sight of peace and joy. But there is a contrast to this hectic pace, a time when the world feels still, and everything slows down for just a moment.

There is something extraordinary about the simple serenity of the very early morning that cannot be found at any other time. Though it is extremely difficult to roll out of bed, the mesh of the still of night and the soft glow of morning brings me solace. My daughter is sleeping soundly, dreams permeated with swimming in buckets of chocolate candies, jumping on the trampoline while the fall leaves bounce with her, or one day having a YouTube channel where she can rate Starbucks drinks or Crumbl cookies (I guess that is the current rage these days).

The light from the diffuser provides a simple ambiance that gives off the calmness I need for the long day ahead. My coffee can be sipped slowly, providing me with a beautiful burn on the tip of my tongue. Flipping open my beautifully worn Bible, a stirring happens within me before I even reach a word. I know that whatever comes my way in the next twenty-four hours can be conquered.

Without a doubt, our tranquility does not come from getting up ridiculously early in the morning, but it can be a catalyst for ultimate peace. When a Bible can be opened without interruption, a conversation with Jesus can happen freely. It is where peace can be acknowledged and invited into our day before the day begins. The idea of a prayerful morning is not only a domino choice that can literally improve your entire day; it is a biblical concept.

There are numerous instances in both the Old and New Testament where judges, prophets, disciples, and even kings rose early to pray or listen to God's voice. One of whom was King David, a man loved deeply by God and even named a "man after [God's] own heart" (Acts 13:22). Connecting with the Maker not only set the tone for King David's day but also positioned him to lead with wisdom and humility. Even as a king with immense power, David understood that true strength came not from his royal title but from his reliance on the Lord.

> When a Bible can be opened without interruption, a conversation with Jesus can happen freely.

In the quiet moments of the morning, before the chaos of his responsibilities began, David made it a priority to commune with God. This intimate time with the Creator allowed him to ground himself in His presence, preparing his heart for the challenges ahead. David's daily rhythm was centered on two powerful practices: offering prayers and hearing God's word. Just as David heard God's voice in his life, we too have the opportunity to hear from God through the written Word He has given us. David shares with us, "In the morning, Lord, you hear my voice; in the morning I lay my requests before you and wait expectantly" (Psalm 5:3 NIV). David knew that in order to be a good king, he would need to seek God first.

David did not approach the day with self-sufficiency, but with an open heart, longing to hear from God. He understood that spending time with God was the right path for success (even if he still chose to make some not-so-good decisions). In Psalm 119:147, David says, "I rise before the dawning of the morning, and cry for help; I hope in Your word." His rising early was not merely a routine but an expression of his deep yearning for God's direction and strength. The word of God, for David, was a lifeline that sustained him throughout the day, providing wisdom, comfort, and clarity as a ruler.

Even as king, David never outgrew his need for God's wisdom. His dependence on God was unwavering; he knew that his power as king was secondary to his position as a servant of the Lord. Through prayer and hearing God's word, David set the stage, not just for his leadership, but for his entire life. This humble reliance on God was the foundation of his kingship, reminding us that true leadership comes from a heart that seeks God first.

David was not the only one who knew the importance of seeking God early. Like David, Moses also began his day by turning to God. Moses writes, "Satisfy us in the morning with your unfailing love, that we may sing for joy and be glad all our days" (Psalm 90:14 NIV). Not only would Moses have a clearer structure for his day by seeking God first, but his priorities would also be more spiritually aligned.

Pastor and evangelist F. B. Meyer also reminds us that, "There is no hour like that of morning prime for fellowship with God. If we would dare to wait before Him for satisfaction then, the filling of that hour would overflow into all other hours."[1] Both Moses and Meyer recognized that true fulfillment was not found in wealth, fame, romance, pleasure, or success. Instead, it stemmed from God's mercy and His unwavering faithfulness to us that could be best seen if a believer dedicated time in the morning to our Lord and Savior. Moses understood that his spirit needed to be filled with God and not anything else that may tempt us. It is only His love that keeps us grounded.

Have you not seen God's faithfulness time and time again in your own life when you ensure quiet time with Him? On the days when you put God first, you can look back and see that your totally unmanageable days become a little more manageable. Perhaps your teenager squeezes you in an unanticipated hug. Perhaps your check deposits a day early, covering your electric bill. Making time for God first will not take away the tiredness you already feel after getting the kids off to school, but you are able to take a deep breath that stills your heart, soul, and mind because you have spent time with your Savior first. It is not just best to go to God in the morning. Momma, you need Him first.

As a single mother, there are many days when it feels like you do not have the energy to wake up any earlier than you already have to. There are days when your heart is in a state of brokenness, unable to even speak. You often find yourself getting to bed later than planned, only to struggle with falling asleep because of worry or uneasiness. It can be all too easy to move your early alarm to a later time or turn

Imagine what could happen if you trusted in His mathematics and not the mathematics of your human brain.

it off completely. This is when you need to wake even earlier to reach out to God and share with Him a prayer of deep affliction. Though it may appear counterproductive in your mathematical thinking—to wake up earlier when you are exhausted—you know that God is not a one plus one equals two sort of God. He is a one plus one equals three Father. Imagine what could happen if you trusted in His mathematics and not the mathematics of your human brain.

Reach out to God before all things. Connect with Him before the sun rises, before the demanding day starts, before even the tears are allowed to begin. It does not need to be hours, only minutes.

For me, waking up thirty minutes earlier than necessary works best. It gives me enough time to use the bathroom, brew my espresso, and settle in for fifteen to twenty minutes of uninterrupted quiet time. When my daughter was a baby, my only choice was to wake up early to ensure I had that moment with God. As she grew, I trained her so that when she sees me at the kitchen table with my Bible open, she can hug me, but she knows not to interrupt unless it is an emergency.

One step toward God can turn into an entire staircase. Little did I know that these few moments with Jesus would not only affect my day ahead, but my daughter too. As a ten-year-old, she now wakes up on her own and spends a few moments with God too. Then, she independently prepares for the day while I finish up my moments with God. It has been an honor to watch her spiritually grow.

As a single momma, your days are overflowing with little hands to guide, meals to prepare, messes to clean, and hearts to nurture. In the midst of all the noise and needs, it can be hard to stay close to Jesus. The beautiful truth is that He is not asking for perfection. He only desires presence with you. Here are a few grace-filled steps you can take throughout your day to intentionally turn your heart toward Jesus.

Go to God in the morning. Choose the amount of time you would like to spend with your Father and set your alarm to go off early enough to have that time. Allow a few extra minutes for a face wash, a coffee, or some ice water that will aid in waking you. Starting your day with God sets the tone for everything that follows. It reminds your heart who is in control and centers your mind on what truly matters. This intentional time creates space for peace before the rush begins, and it opens your spirit to hear His voice before the world gets loud.

Arrange your thoughts and requests to God. Think about how you would like to spend your time with your Father. Is it reading a few verses in your Bible, a plan on the Bible app, or a devotional? Find what works best for you and be sure there is a mixture of His Word to you and your word to Him in prayer. Consider keeping a journal nearby to write down what you're learning, what you're praying for, or simply how you're feeling. This helps you track your spiritual growth and see God's faithfulness over time. Let this be a conversation, not a ritual—an honest, living connection with the One who loves you most.

Take Jesus with you throughout your day. One way to take your morning devotion time into your day is to choose a Bible verse or a powerful statement that you start each morning off with and eventually memorize. I call this my Jesus Statement. It is a simple step, but it becomes the anchor of my heart as I begin each day. When life starts to feel overwhelming and chaotic, having a go-to statement ready reminds me of my foundation and brings me back to the peace I need.

My Jesus Statement is something I intentionally read first thing every morning, and it stays with me for months at a time, shifting as my circumstances change. Currently, the verse that I am holding on to is Psalm 23:1: "The Lord is my shepherd, I lack nothing." (NIV). It is written on a weathered index card that is tucked inside my Bible as a bookmark, and I also keep a second copy on the mirror of my SUV.

This simple verse has become an anchor for me. Every time I see it, it serves as a powerful reminder that, no matter what I face throughout the day, I have already been equipped with everything I need to navigate it. The Lord is with me, guiding me, so I do not have to worry or feel anxious. I can circle in His peace and stillness instead of getting caught in the cycle of worry. I have everything I need in this very moment.

As teacher Charles Spurgeon wisely said, "He who is diligent in prayer will never be destitute of hope. Observe that as the early bird gets the worm, the early prayer is soon refreshed with hope."[2] The discipline of starting my day with the Lord not only strengthens my connection to Him but also refreshes my hope, no matter what the day holds.

I am learning more each day that it is in those quiet moments of reflection, rooted in Scripture and prayer, that I find the hope and calm I need to face whatever comes my way. May we walk together in that same expectation today, knowing that our foundation is secure and we are held by the One who knows us best.

Prayer

A Prayer for the Morning

*Heavenly Father,
as I rise each morning, I seek Your
guidance to establish a routine
that honors You and reflects Your love
in my life. Help me to prioritize
moments of prayer and reflection and
to embrace the day with gratitude and
purpose. May each action be a
testament to Your grace, drawing
me closer to You and allowing me
to shine Your light in all I do.
Strengthen my resolve and fill my heart
with joy as I dedicate my morning
and day to Your glory.
Amen.*

Bible

Scriptures for Preparing the Heart

But I cry to you for help, Lord; in the morning my prayer comes before you.
Psalm 88:13

Because of the Lord's great love we are not consumed, for his compassions never fail. They are new every morning; great is your faithfulness. I say to myself, 'The Lord is my portion; therefore I will wait for him.'
Lamentations 3:22-24

This is the day the Lord has made. We will rejoice and be glad in it.
Psalm 118:24 NLT

Verses

Scriptures for Preparing the Heart

O God, You are my God;
Early will I seek You; My soul thirsts for You;
My flesh longs for You In a dry and thirsty
land where there is no water.
Psalm 63:1 NKJV

But I will sing of your strength,
in the morning I will sing of your love;
for you are my fortress, my refuge
in times of trouble.
Psalm 59:16

My voice You shall hear
in the morning, O Lord;
In the morning I will direct it to You,
And I will look up.
Psalm 5:3

Chapter Two

PEACE AT HOME

My stomach churned harder with each passing mile on my way to work.

I had never truly fit in there. I did things differently, not wrongly, just differently. My work ethic has always been guided by Colossians 3:23: "Whatever you do, work at it with all your heart, as working for the Lord" (NIV). Meeting my job requirements was not a necessity—exceeding them was. And well, it caused a ruckus.

I stuck out, like a person dressed in a bright yellow dress at a funeral. My department was growing—reaching new heights with my unique leadership management—and administration had noticed. They did not notice my astounding increase in usage of the department area or the expansion of new programs. They did not notice that I would be one of the first in my office in the mornings and oftentimes had a working lunch if it meant the department would run more smoothly. They did notice, however, that I did not fit in their box. So much so that I was invited to a meeting where I would be put on a PIP plan. That is right, a Performance Improvement Plan—while overseeing a department that was growing exponentially. Makes sense, right? Not so much.

Because of that meeting, work no longer felt as safe as it used to—hence the stomach churning as another day began. My time at work no longer felt like a catalyst for change but like walking on nails. A once harmonious place where I saw myself for the long term was now filled with disharmony, uncertainty, and unknowns for the future.

It is certain that the future will be uncertain.

Just like I could not change the uncertainty or the stresses I now felt at work, I could not control when my tire went flat or the extra high heating bill that further lowered my dwindling bank account. I could not control my ex-husband, who had freely given me full custody yet desired to break me. After all, it is certain that the future will be uncertain. Although I knew my problems could not be solved instantly, I wanted to find a place of peace, not just from the difficulties of being a single mother, but from all the difficulties of the world. I wanted a safety net to come home to that provided me tranquility and serenity in a world of chaos as a single momma. I wanted consistency in an inconsistent world. I did not just desire a place of solace; I needed one.

No matter how we reached single motherhood, it was undoubtedly a grueling and agonizing experience. Whether we came to be a single mother through divorce, a broken relationship, a death, or by choice, becoming a mother on our own is not an easy process. The mental strength we have is tested. Many of us may have even been broken from the hurts of this broken word, sending us to a long-term state of chaos. We are desperate for a refuge.

As a believer, we automatically have a sanctuary specifically pre-pared for us. This special dwelling place, this "secret place" (Psalm 91:1), is not only reserved but is always open, available for us to seek refuge in at any moment. Psalms remind us of this truth: "He who dwells in the secret place of the Most High shall abide under the shadow of the Almighty" (v. 1). When we choose to dwell with God, living in constant communion with Him through patience in reading His Word, prayer, and persistent action, we discover a profound sense of protection and peace that only He can provide. Under His wing, we find a safety and a care that no other place can offer. The result? A deep confidence in God's protection that is unmatched and unwavering.

The unknown psalmist continues to boldly declare, "He is my refuge and my fortress; my God, in Him I will trust" (Psalm 91:2). The writer places his full reliance on God, trusting that God is his safe haven, an impenetrable defense. Similarly, our safe haven in God is not just a refuge we turn to in times of trouble but a constant, reliable source of protection and care that is always available to us. By choosing to live in constant communion with Him, we too are wrapped in His sheltering presence, which offers us rest, security, and peace at all times.

As believing mommas, we already know that Jesus is our safe haven. The problem is that we have heard this truth so often that it risks becoming more of a cliché than a genuine, life-changing reality. Do we truly believe that we can run to Him at any time, in any circumstance, and not only receive His protection but also His unwavering love.

In the chaos of motherhood, where our patience runs thin, our hearts are stretched, and our strength feels depleted, do we really choose to take refuge in His presence? Have we allowed the busyness of life to dull the significance of what it means to be held and comforted by the Creator of the universe while living as single mommas? Jesus invites us to bring our burdens to Him, to rest in His stillness, and to trust in His provision while living a faith-filled life directed toward Him; but it does take effort on our part.

Just as building a physical house requires careful planning, thoughtful design, and the coordination of materials, workers, and details, the construction of our spiritual home does too. It takes thoughtful planning and diligence to build a life grounded in godly wisdom and strength. The wonderful news is that when we put in the effort to prioritize God, even in the midst of the chaos of children, work, and daily responsibilities, He blesses us. Proverbs 24 states, "By wisdom a house is built, and through understanding it is established; through knowledge its rooms are filled with rare and beautiful treasures" (Proverbs 24:3–4 NIV). I love the commentary with this verse, "The precious jewels that fill the house are a harmonious, loving family and a sense of security and stability."[3] Oh, how we, as single mothers, long for these rare earthly treasures of safety, protection, and strength. The beautiful truth is that these blessings are not only possible but readily available to us. In fact, as believers, it is already within us through the Holy Spirit.

In the same way, our sanctuary, our refuge in Christ, is inseparable from us because of our belief in Him. The Holy Spirit is our constant, quietly present even when we may not fully recognize it. Our need is simply to acknowledge Him, to remember that we carry this sacred place with us wherever we go, and to walk in such a way because we know He is within us. Our true Refuge is never far, always available, and always near.

When we enter His dwelling place, we are in a permanent place of safety in an impermanent world. We are near to Him, receiving his protection and peace. It means we have a place of peace in the midst of chaos. A place of ultimate rest from stressful workplaces, people who drain us, or exes who just do not understand us. Profound protection and peace are found in God's presence.

The more I discovered an ever-present spiritual refuge for my soul, the stronger my desire grew to make my "secret place of the Most High" (Psalm 91:1) not just a distant spiritual goal but a tangible reality in my daily life.

Though I may not be trained in architecture or home construction, I have the ability to take deliberate steps to make my home a sanctuary of peace, security, and stability.

When we enter His dwelling place, we are in a permanent place of safety in an impermanent world.

The rental duplex we used to stay in had a very rental vibe. The white walls and the metal accessible bar by the toilet hinted that this home was not mine. A part of me hesitated to decorate because I was not ready to make the space feel permanent. Yet deep down, I knew that if I wanted to create a sanctuary of godly rest amid the chaos, I had to take action and make it happen. And so, the process of cleansing and decorating began.

Anything that did not bring me joy was quickly listed on Facebook Marketplace, especially items that stirred painful memories. This included a nearly brand-new Apple iPad—a gift from our last anniversary before the divorce—and my wedding ring, the one I had worn for only a few months, that I had been staring at for nearly ten years. My makeshift office, technically a walk-in closet, felt all the more spacious when a few clothing brackets were taken down. I bought turquoise and dark gray curtains and wall décor in soothing colors that brought me joy and comfort.

It was not easy for me, as it meant spending money I had saved for future emergencies. But in black-and-white, perhaps it was an emergency. For my mental well-being, creating a space where I could come home and truly feel at ease needed to be a priority. Who would have thought that something as simple as a few fabric panels and curtain rods could contribute so much to a better state of mind while aiding in a spiritually safe place?

I invested in a distressed white and gray letter board, where I could put rotating Bible verses that would bring me a visual go-to when I needed a boost of consolation in the midst of boiling macaroni noodles or cleaning out the birdcage (it is usually my Jesus Statement from chapter 1). My daughter was thrilled to have a light box in her room to display her own Jesus-inspired messages. She carefully crafted her favorite Bible verses on index cards, decorated them with markers and glitter, then hung them up with vibrant strings in her favorite colors. Meanwhile, I started diffusing essential oils regularly in the main areas of the house, always keeping worship music softly playing in the background in the mornings. Slowly, I transformed our home into a physical and spiritual haven, a place of refuge and calmness. As I made these changes, I could feel my heart being drawn closer to God in new ways—each small act became an offering to Him, a way to invite His peace into our daily lives. Even in the busiest moments, I found myself pausing to breathe in deeply, sensing His presence in the quiet corners of our home.

These thoughtful touches began to shape the atmosphere around us, reminding us that our home was not just a physical space, but a place where God's peace could settle. I also found that having a calm, focused environment made it easier to hear His voice, to pray, and to reflect on His Word during even the most ordinary tasks. The more I created space for worship and Scripture in our home, the more I noticed how much my heart longed to be centered on Him—how it became less about the external decor and more about cultivating an inner peace that mirrored His love. These small, intentional changes became more than just decor—they became daily reminders of God's nearness. In the quiet rhythms of ordinary life, I began to feel His peace more deeply: in the scent of lavender filling the air, in the quiet lyrics drifting from the kitchen, and in the flicker of truth on a letter board or index card. The soft hum of worship music became like a constant prayer, a soundtrack of gratitude that anchored me throughout the day. Our home did not need to be perfect—it just needed to point us back to Jesus. And little by little, that's exactly what it began to do.

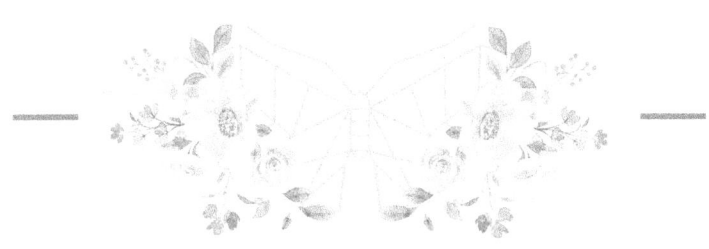

As a strong single momma in the midst of chaos, what steps can you take to make your physical home a more spiritual home? Here are a few things on which to reflect:

- Are there items in your home that are not being used that can be decluttered?

- Do the colors in your home calm you or agitate you?

- What visuals on your walls or counters direct you to Him?

- Is there something your children can craft by hand or on the computer that will encourage them spiritually in their rooms?

- What items can be purchased to promote a more calming haven?

Make small steps to reach the goal of a spiritually and physically peaceful home. Depending on your budget, you might consider adding a calming accent wall or a piece with an inspiring quote. Above my bed, for example, I have a black-and-white cursive sign that declares "Give it to God and go to sleep." The sign serves as a powerful reminder that no matter how the day has gone, I can take a deep breath and release it all to God—even if only for a moment.

It is truly amazing how these small changes can transform your space into a peaceful sanctuary, one that not only beautifies your home but also spiritually encourages you during those difficult workdays. Even a simple addition like a cozy reading corner, a few scented candles, or soft lighting can shift the energy of a room, helping you unwind and reconnect with what matters most. Over time, these intentional touches will further support your place of refuge—a reminder that peace is always possible.

My home is my spiritual safe haven. Every time I enter my home, no matter what happens in my day, there is rest within my soul and within my home. Though problems are still there, though hard things are still hard, peace greets me at home. Though work or other parts of the outside world may attempt to break me, my front door is where the world cannot cross. It can be the same for you too.

No matter how unsafe the world may feel, how chaotic the work-place might be, or how challenging our days can become, we always have the ability to create a sanctuary of peace and safety within our own homes. In a world that often feels unstable, our homes can be places of refuge, physical spaces that reflect the deep spiritual safety we find in our Lord.

Shalom, my dear mommas.

Prayer

A Prayer for Peace

Dear Lord,
I come before You asking
for Your divine help in creating
a peaceful home for myself and my children.
Surround us with Your love and tranquility,
guiding us to communicate with
kindness and understanding.
May our home be a sanctuary filled with joy,
laughter, and warmth, where Your
presence is felt in every moment.
Help us to nurture one another, fostering
an environment of love and safety.
I trust in Your wisdom to lead us,
so that our family may grow together
in harmony and faith.
Amen.

Bible

Scriptures of Peaceful Promises

For every house is built by someone,
but God is the builder of everything.
Hebrews 3:4

Unless the Lord builds the house,
the builders labor in vain.
Unless the Lord watches over the city,
the guards stand watch in vain.
Psalm 127:1

My people will live in peaceful
dwelling places, in secure homes,
in undisturbed places of rest.
Isaiah 32:18

You will be blessed when you come in
and blessed when you go out.
Deuteronomy 28:6

Verses

Scriptures of Peaceful Promises

Through wisdom a house is built,
And by understanding it is established;
By knowledge the rooms are filled
With all precious and pleasant riches.
Proverbs 24:3-4

But if serving the Lord
seems undesirable to you, then
choose for yourselves this day
whom you will serve,
whether the gods your ancestors
served beyond the Euphrates,
or the gods of the Amorites,
in whose land you are living.
But as for me and my household,
we will serve the Lord.
Joshua 24:15

Beautiful
Messiness

Chapter Three
Organized Chaos

Did you know my daughter's diorama was due yesterday? You may think that perhaps she totally forgot to make me aware of this detailed project. Absolutely not! We spent days on that designer diorama. The shoebox consisted of green cardstock walls decorated with bamboo and fern trees. Popsicle sticks mimicked bamboo shoots and construction paper became frilly green grass. In the middle of the box sat the cutest black-and-white panda, handcrafted with air-dry clay, eyes wide, belly bulging. Blood, sweat, and tears were put into the diorama so that my daughter could present to her class her favorite animal and its environment. Lamentably, the project sat stoically on the wooden kitchen table when it was supposed to be sitting on her desk at school.

It was not the first time I forgot a due date or a planned event. Just last Sunday, I completely forgot about my daughter's "Jam Team" practice at church. This was her chance to learn the songs and moves for children's worship, but I missed it. A month ago, we had signed up for a painting project at the local library, but I forgot all about it. Even worse, picture day rolled around, and it was one of those rare mornings when we did not manage to comb her hair or coordinate her outfit. To this day, she still teases me about her messy hair and mismatched clothes. Do your kids ever remind you of your forgetfulness? They remember the smallest details, don't they? Even the things we thought they'd forget.

The problem is that I often try to be a Cirque-du-Soleil mom—juggling it all and pushing myself to be 110 percent everything to everyone. I do not want my daughter to feel the absence of a two-parent home, so I say yes to nearly every commitment, activity, or responsibility. I try to fill every gap to ensure she never feels deprived. As a parent, I don't want her to experience hardship, especially hardships that were not of her making. But in my effort to shield her from pain, I sometimes stretch myself too thin.

Are you the same too?

Do you say yes to absolutely everything, even if it means you are the one to take the brunt of what is left? Perhaps it is purchasing something for your son that you know he dearly wants even though you know it means working extra hours to make up for what you should not have bought. Perhaps it is volunteering to bake cookies for a church fundraiser on the same day your daughter has T-ball practice in another town, which means missing some of her practice because you have to deliver them. Perhaps you said yes to an extra job because you know you need the money for a family vacation you want to take your kids on, and it may mean missing Sunday service. Your schedule is jam-packed because there is just not another option, or perhaps is there?

Not only is it exhausting to manage a never-ending list of tasks, events, and obligations, it is also ineffective and unwise for long-term success, both for you and your family. Moses, in his prayer, writes, "So teach us to number our days, that we may gain a heart of wisdom" (Psalm 90:12). As the leader of Israel, Moses had far more than a simple to-do list. He was managing what felt like an unending pile of responsibilities. He was in charge of millions of people. His days were packed from morning to night, overseeing numerous leaders from all twelve tribes, ensuring the tabernacle was properly maintained, and most importantly, communicating with God about the nation's challenges. And that is only a glimpse of his responsibilities. Even Moses, with all his leadership experience, recognized that he needed divine wisdom to navigate the overwhelming demands of each day.

While in the wilderness Moses requested, "Teach us" (v. 12). In his difficult circumstances, Moses requested for true wisdom, not just a simple one-time answer that may help him in the moment. He desired to do better, to use his days more wisely, to "number [his] days" (v. 12). It is not just about acknowledging life's fleeting nature but about learning to live with purpose and intention in the limited time we have, making choices that reflect God's wisdom in everything we do. We should also ask God for the wisdom to recognize how fleeting our time is and to learn to number our days, making each one count.

> *It is not just about acknowledging life's fleeting nature but about learning to live with purpose and intention in the limited time we have.*

We can read more about Moses's difficulty with managing his day in Exodus 18, where Moses's father-in-law, Jethro, advised him to delegate responsibilities to other leaders in order to better manage the community. Jethro saw that Moses was overwhelmed with the weight of overseeing the entire nation of Israel on his own and suggested that he appoint capable leaders to share the burden.

If Moses, someone who communicated directly with God, needed wisdom and support to handle his responsibilities, it is a powerful reminder that we, too, need leadership, guidance, and wisdom in our own lives. We were never meant to carry burdens alone. Just as Moses relied on God's wisdom and the counsel of others, we should also seek the help and wisdom we need to navigate our own challenges. If Moses needed leaders and wisdom, do you not think we need it too?

We can gain more knowledge in the book of Proverbs, where King Solomon, known for his wisdom, reminds us that, before we move forward with anything, we must first properly prepare. Proverbs 24:27 states, "Prepare your outside work, make it fit for yourself in the field; and afterward build your house." Before building a house, careful preparations are necessary. The land must first be prepared and made ready before a house with a strong foundation is built. In other words, a well-thought-out plan with clear steps is essential if we want to see a fruitful harvest. By planning thoroughly and taking careful steps, we set ourselves up for success and ensure that what we build is spiritually secure and sustainable.

As single mothers, staying organized is essential, not just for our own sanity, but also for the well-being of our children. With so many demands on our time—multiple jobs, house chores, financial responsibilities, and being there emotionally for our children—it is easy for the mental restlessness to spill into our physical everyday lives. The pressure can feel overwhelming, and it can be hard to find balance amidst it all. However, by taking the time to prepare and being patient with both ourselves and our children, we lay the foundation for a more successful daily life.

This approach not only helps us manage our current responsibilities but also creates the potential for building toward larger dreams and goals in the future. Additionally, fostering a sense of order in our homes, rather than allowing chaos to reign, gives us the mental space we need to care for ourselves, recharge, and be more present for our children. In doing so, we are ultimately supporting our emotional well-being and creating a nurturing environment for our family to thrive in.

A well-organized home provides much-needed consistency and stability for our children. When children know what to expect each day, they feel safer and more secure. Keeping things organized, whether it is meal planning, school schedules, or bedtime routines, creates a stable environment where our children can thrive. It also allows us to model essential life skills, such as time management, responsibility, and the importance of planning ahead. By setting a structured environment, we are teaching our children how to approach their own responsibilities with confidence and discipline. In this way, our organization does more than help us survive the day; it equips our children with the tools they need to succeed in their own lives, showing them the value of order, consistency, and forward-thinking.

Prayer is how we speak to God, and the Bible is how He speaks to us.

Where and how do we even begin? We can gain renewed wisdom through communication with God. Prayer is how we speak to God, and the Bible is how He speaks to us. What does the Bible say about being organized? We can flip to the very first page of the Bible to see God's organization in Genesis. Check out God's first earthly schedule:

Day 1: God creates light.

Day 2: God creates the sky.

Day 3: God creates dry land, plants, and seas.

Day 4: God creates the sun, moon, and stars.

Day 5: God creates water and sky animals.

Day 6: God creates land animals and people.

Day 7: God rests from His work and calls it holy.

He took the chaos of this universe and brought order, setting a purposeful pattern where each day had its own unique creation, yet each day built upon the one before. We, too, can find order in the chaos of our lives as single mommas. The demands on our time can often feel overwhelming, balancing work, household responsibilities, and emotional support for our children, but structure can improve our household. By creating small systems and organizing our days, we can transform the chaos into a space of peace and productivity.

Having order does not mean everything will be perfect or controlled (after all, Adam and Eve eventually committed the first human sin despite living on a perfect earth), but it does mean we have a sense of direction amid the busyness. When we have structure, we can make better decisions. Just as God established a purposeful plan for each day, we can establish routines that serve our needs and bring stability to our homes.

What steps can you take today to create more structure, organization, and peace in your life, turning the messy chaos into a place of organized chaos for both you and your children? Remember, even small changes can lead to big transformations over time. Here are a few things that work for my little family.

Purchase a Physical Calendar

Buy a physical calendar, along with a ridiculously large package of colorful thin line markers that includes a red. Not an online calendar or app. A physical paper calendar that can be put in a central area in your home for everyone in the family to see. When one of your beautiful children asks about plans, you can direct them to the calendar. Perhaps your children want to go to the playground or the local skating rink. The family can come together by the calendar and choose a date. Not only will a calendar provide more consistency and routine to them, but fewer questions asked to you!

Meal Plan and Prep

Incorporating a few hours into your schedule where you plan and prep meals for the following week will not only keep you organized, it will keep your stress at bay. Utilizing online grocery apps for quick pickup and having your older children help you prep food will ease the stress throughout the week—and it is a great way to bond. If possible, preparing a few dishes over the weekend for the week will stretch your minutes. If your children pack their lunch during the week, prepping snack packs of fruits, cheeses, and other items that can be quickly grabbed out of the fridge is immensely helpful for morning times.

Incorporate Rest Days

Mark two days each month with a red X to designate them as 'Nothing Days.' These are days for you and your family to completely disconnect from work, chores, and obligations. It is a day dedicated to rest and enjoyment, with the benefit of both you and your children recharging. If a picnic in the park sounds like fun, do it—whatever brings you and your family joy. Keep in mind, we have the other twenty-eight days in the month to tackle the to-do list, drive kids to activities, and stay productive. These 'Nothing Days' are meant for a time for you to recharge and your children to rest, and if you make them nonnegotiable, you will be amazed by the positive impact they have on your well-being and family life.

In reality, two days of rest is often not enough. Finding additional days—or even just a few hours—to rest physically at home can bring much-needed mental clarity and foster long-term peace within your family. Another way to incorporate more rest into your routine is by embracing the spiritual renewal of the Sabbath. Taking time to rest on a Saturday or Sunday within your home can provide a unique blessing, nurturing both your soul and your family's well-being.

What may seem like an unconventional approach to one family could be exactly what is needed in yours. For example, perhaps requiring all your children, including your busy high schooler, to stay home on Sundays might seem extreme to some, but it could be the crucial downtime your family needs to recharge after an exhausting week. The other six days may be packed with obligations, leaving everyone drained, and a day of rest could help restore balance. Whatever you choose, make clear-cut steps to move from messy to manageable. You got this, momma.

Prayer

A Prayer for Order

Dear Lord,
I ask for Your guidance
in my daily life, that each moment
may be filled with purpose and
dedicated to Your glory. Help me to
recognize the opportunities
You place before me, so I can serve
others and reflect Your love in every
interaction. Grant me the wisdom
to use my time wisely,
making choices that honor You and
spread Your light. May my thoughts, words,
and actions be aligned with Your will, and
may I find joy in living each
day as an offering to You.
Amen.

Bible

Scriptures on Order

*For God is not a God of disorder
but of peace—as in all the
congregations of the Lord's people.
1 Corinthians 14:33*

*Prepare your outside work,
make it fit for yourself in the field;
and afterward build your house.
Proverbs 24:27*

*She watches over the ways of her household,
And does not eat the bread of idleness.
Proverbs 31:27*

*But everything should be done
in a fitting and orderly way.
1 Corinthians 14:40 NIV*

Verses

Scriptures on Order

Commit your works to the LORD,
and your thoughts will be established.
Proverbs 16:3

You shall bring in the table
and arrange the things that are
to be set in order on it;
and you shall bring in the
lampstand and light its lamps.
Exodus 40:4

For though I am absent in the flesh,
yet I am with you in spirit,
rejoicing to see your good order
and the steadfastness of
your faith in Christ.
Colossians 2:5

Forward
Focus

Chapter Four
PURPOSEFUL PLANNING

"Mom, what are we doing this weekend?" my little one asks, her voice high-pitched and full of eager expectation.

"I don't know, sweetie. It just depends on things," I reply, trying to sound assuring as I swing open the heavy car door, ready to tackle the numerous bags of food. I gently help her out of the deep plum SUV.

"Can we go to the park by the pool? And . . . and . . . also go to the dollar store so I can spend the money I saved?" she pleads, her eyes bright with excitement, hands clasped tightly around her little pink and orange backpack full of pennies, nickels, and dimes she earned from chores.

"We just came from a store, honey. We will see about the park," I answer, attempting to sound like I have it all figured out. I grab all five grocery bags, their weight pulling my arm down, being careful not to let the watermelon in my left arm slip.

"I really want to go, Mom!" she says, her voice growing more insistent. I can feel her little feet scuffing the pavement beside me, the impatience in her steps matching the urgency in her tone.

My own uneasiness starts to creep in, like a tightening knot in my chest. "Honey, I do not know what we are having for dinner tonight, let alone what we will be doing this weekend. Let me think about it, and I will let you know." I attempt to mask my uncertainty with a smile that does not quite reach my eyes.

"But Mmmoooommm!" she whines, her frustration bubbling over as she stomps her foot with all the defiance of a tween wannabe, trying to assert her growing independence. It's moments like these that remind me just how unpredictable life can be, leaving me feeling stretched thin as I try to manage both her emotions and my own.

This constant juggling of responsibilities only adds to the overwhelming sense of uncertainty in my life. The idea of having clear-cut goals does not exactly sound thrilling to me. With all the demands of being a single parent, it is hard enough to maintain any sense of structure in the present, let alone set my sights on some distant future idea. The thought of creating elaborate plans or striving toward big ambitions seems almost out of reach when just making it through the day without losing my sanity feels like an achievement in itself.

Some days, just surviving the constant juggling act of work, school runs, meal prep, and emotional support feels like more than enough. The idea of adding future goals on top of that feels overwhelming and, honestly, impossible as I am already stretched thin and barely holding it all together.

A part of me desires to be one of those parents who can breeze through the years of motherhood without a care in the world and still keep my sanity. You know, those hippie-like moms who are truly zen in the disorderly days. It appears so much easier if I would stop caring about a schedule for the present and ambitions to look forward to. After all, who needs goals? They feel like an extra, unnecessary source of stress.

It may sound more manageable to just wing single motherhood, but it could potentially turn us into mommas on the verge of insanity. The chaos, the unpredictability—it is all part of the ride of single motherhood, but who really wants to be on a ride that never stops spinning? Do we not want more than insanity? Do we not want a sense of purpose, some kind of road map to guide us through the madness and provide us affirmation that we are on the right path, despite it being a bumpy road?

I desire to not just have plans, but to have a clear direction. I want to know that even when everything feels out of control in my single motherhood, I am still moving toward something meaningful, even if it is just small steps. When it feels like I have failed as a mother and leader of my family, those are the moments when my God-directed goals become my anchor. Goals help me center myself, even if just for a moment, and remind me that life is not just about surviving the chaos. However unclear at the moment, it is about much more: keeping my eyes on that horizon of God-ordained future.

> When it feels like I have failed as a mother and leader of my family, those are the moments when my god-directed goals become my anchor.

King Solomon provides us with a multitude of advice about leading well with plans. Proverbs 21:5 says, "The plans of the diligent lead surely to plenty, but those of everyone who is hasty, surely to poverty." When we carefully plan and pair it with dedicated effort, the results are abundant. In other words, when we plan, God will bless those plans.

The opposite can be true too. If we choose to hurriedly move through our daily lives, it will not bring success and may in fact bring not-so-good consequences to too-quick reactions. Taking shortcuts or failing to do things the right way can set us back instead of moving us forward. As the verse warns, those who act hastily may experience poverty, not prosperity.

I know, momma, it may feel like an enormous obstacle to overcome. The word poverty can be unsettling. Those seven letters together have the power to stir up a deep sense of fear and anxiety within me. They shoot straight to my soul, triggering thoughts of struggle and uncertainty. The idea of not having enough, to perhaps even forever struggle, overwhelms me. It feels as though the weight of the world is suddenly pressing down on me, making everything seem so much harder than it already is. And it scares me beyond words.

If you limit god, He has no choice but to limit what He does through you.

Can I be honest with you? For many years, I went through my days without giving much thought to the future. There were times when I worked up to four jobs, yet I had no clear direction for where my life was headed, or even where my money was going. I was just focused on surviving each day. I did not feel the need to look any further ahead. It was easier to stay in the moment than to confront the uncertainty that lay ahead.

Part of that was fear—fear that I wanted things I did not believe a single mother could achieve. But a bigger part was that I was not planning for the future at all. I was holding myself back, and in doing so, I was also limiting what God could do in my life. If you limit God, He has no choice but to limit what He does through you. I have come to realize that I desire to live a life without limitations—a life shaped by vision, not fear. Don't you?

We must ensure that our plans align not only with our own desires but also with God's sovereign purpose for our family.

While it is natural to want what we think is best for ourselves, we must remember that God, in His infinite wisdom, sees the bigger picture. He is all-powerful and all-knowing, and His plan for our lives far surpasses any path we might choose, no matter how strongly we feel about our own desires. Proverbs 16:9 reminds us, "A man's heart plans his way, but the Lord directs his steps." This verse is not saying our plans are inherently bad, but rather, God's plans are infinitely better. As the Creator of everything, including us, God knows every step and outcome of our lives, which makes it essential to seek His direction rather than relying solely on our limited understanding.

When we recognize the depth of God's wisdom and the beauty of His plan for our lives, it becomes clear that aligning ourselves with Him is the wisest choice we can make. If He is the maker of all things and knows the path ahead, why would we choose to walk alone? It only makes sense to approach our plans with humility, surrendering them to God's will. Personally, I would much rather have God's best plan for my life than even my own good plan. After all, His will is perfect, and by trusting in Him, we position ourselves to experience the fullness of His blessing and purpose for our family. When we trust God with our future, we invite His divine direction and peace, knowing that His plan far exceeds anything we could ever imagine on our own.

We have established that it is valuable to have future goals, but it is also necessary to not forget our purpose. We were created by Him and for Him. If we are not careful, we may reach our goals only to crash and burn, purely because we did not spend time seeking God's guidance on those goals. In this process, it is important to remember that God's timing is as crucial as His plan. We may be eager to rush ahead, but God knows exactly when we are ready for each step. I like Walke's commentary on verse nine, "A man may plan his road to the last detail, but he cannot implement his planning, unless it coincides with Yahweh's plan for him."[4] We must include God in our planning. We must start somewhere.

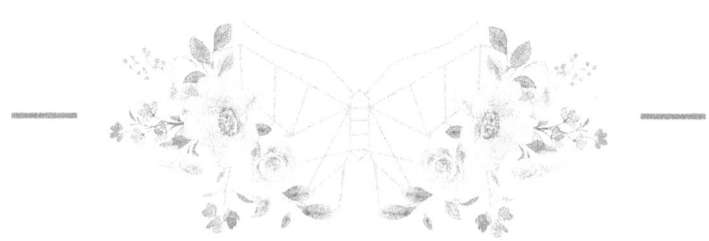

Write down a few possible goals, three short-term and three long-term, that will provide direction for you and your family. Continue to rewrite and hone your goals until you are satisfied with them. This process might take a few days, and that is okay. Let your goals settle in your heart before finalizing them. Here are a few of mine:

Short-Term Goals:

- Dedicate focused, quality time with my daughter during the workweek, prioritizing listening over speaking.

- Journal three to four times a week, reflecting on insights from my therapy sessions.

- Get involved in an upcoming women's Bible study group at church.

Long-Term Goals:

- Increase our family savings with the goal of having six months of emergency funds.

- Start interval training and gradually increase intensity to prepare for completing a 5K race.

- Read through the New Testament in a year, using a commentary for deeper understanding.

Consider the following as you reflect on your goals and intentions:

Are the ambitions and desires I am working toward in harmony with the greater purpose God has designed for me?

When making goals that align with God's purpose for my life, I must first seek His guidance through prayer, trusting that He will direct my steps. I should reflect on the unique gifts, talents, and passions He has given me and set goals that allow me to use them to serve others and fulfill His calling. Last, I need to remain flexible, trusting that God's timing and plan might unfold differently than I expect, and I need to be open to adjusting my goals as I grow in faith and understanding.

Do these current goals fit with my current responsibilities and commitments?

Balancing work, parenting, and household duties requires a careful evaluation of whether my goals are achievable without overwhelming myself. I need to ask if these goals are sustainable within the time and energy I have, or if I am setting myself up for burnout. Ultimately, I want to ensure that my goals support my well-being and my ability to be present for my children, rather than adding unnecessary stress to an already full plate.

Do my goals bring me long-term joy and fulfillment?

I need to ask myself if my goals will bring lasting joy and fulfillment, or if they are just temporary pursuits to something the world says I should work toward. It is important to consider whether my goals help me grow spiritually, emotionally, and personally, or if they leave me feeling empty once achieved. Ultimately, I want to set goals that not only bring success but also a deeper sense of purpose and contentment that lasts beyond the moment.

Once you have created them, place reminders of your goals in multiple spots around your home. I keep a handwritten list in my daily notebook, a printed copy on the wall in my office, and a digital version in my phone's notes. Whenever I have a moment, I review them to see which ones I am making progress on and which ones need more attention. I pray over them regularly, adjusting and refining them as needed. I have found that the more I pray over them, the more my goals shift. They move toward God's plans for me, rather than just my own ambitions.

———————————————

Remember, goals do not promise perfection; they give us inspiration to keep going, even when it feels like everything else is crumbling. In those dark moments, when it seems like we are treading water, our godly goals are the lifeline that helps us stay afloat. They are our reminders that there is more to our story than just the hard days. The bigger picture is still in sight, even if it is only a faint outline for now. Allow time with the Lord to hone those goals, being open to seeing them transform.

Prayer

A Prayer for Direction

Gracious God,
I seek Your guidance as I navigate
my journey and set my goals.
Illuminate the path You have laid
before me, helping me to align my
aspirations with Your will.
Grant me wisdom to discern what
truly glorifies You and the strength to
pursue it with passion and perseverance.
May my ambitions reflect Your love
and grace, serving as a testament
to Your goodness in my life.
Guide my steps, Lord, so that in all I do,
I may honor You and bring hope
to those around me.
Amen.

Bible

Scriptures for Life's Path

Trust in the Lord with all your heart,
And lean not on your own understanding;
In all your ways acknowledge Him,
And He shall direct your paths.
Proverbs 3:5-6

For I know the plans I have for you,
declares the Lord, plans to prosper
you and not to harm you, plans
to give you a hope and a future.
Jeremiah 29:11

In their hearts humans plan their course,
but the Lord establishes their steps.
Proverbs 16:9

Commit to the Lord whatever you do,
and he will establish your plans.
Proverbs 16:3

Verses

Scriptures for Life's Path

Delight yourself also in the Lord,
and He shall give you
the desires of your heart.
Commit your way
to the Lord, trust also in Him,
and He shall bring it to pass.
Psalm 37:4-5

May he give you the desire
of your heart and make all
your plans succeed.
Psalm 20:4

The soul of a lazy man desires,
and has nothing; but the soul
of the diligent shall be made rich.
Proverbs 13:4

Financial Freedom

Chapter Five

MASTER THE HUSTLE

Click. Click. Click. Click.

My heart pounds hard as I log in to my bank account app. I am checking for the third time, as if somehow the numbers might magically change before my eyes. I triple-check everything, hoping that the account balance stays in the black.

Come on! Come oooonnnn! My fingers tremble slightly as I scroll through the screen, eyes locked on the pending transactions, which hang there like a kite caught in the wind, swaying uncontrollably, one wrong gust away from crashing into the red.

I hold my breath as I review each line of pending activity, mentally calculating and recalculating. If everything lines up, if I have timed it right, my account will look like the perfect Tetris game win, pieces slotting into place in perfect harmony. But if it does not work out, if things go sideways, I will be teetering dangerously close to a negative number, a financial cliff that will take my anxiety even higher.

I close my eyes for a moment, telling the number to stay where I need it to. *My pay has been pending forever. Please, just deposit already!* I think it will be okay. I hope it will be. But hope alone will not pay the bills, and the uncertainty gnaws at me, leaving me with a knot in the pit of my stomach that I cannot shake. I can already feel the weight of tomorrow's decisions bearing down on me, the invisible pressure of it all stacking higher than the mountain of receipts and invoices piling up on my kitchen table. I think it will be okay. I think . . . but what if it is not?

Why is there never enough money? As single mommas, we most likely have a few jobs that always just barely cover only the basics, let alone anything else. Despite working multiple jobs or even one with overtime, the bank account just does not display our immensely hard work and sacrifice. We work the extra hours to help save up for an emergency health savings account, and the car breaks go out. We pick up another part-time job to save up for a home to own one day, but then the youngest needs multiple fillings and a crown. The work is never-ending and the bank account is ever-decreasing.

Of all the external struggles that come with single motherhood, finances are the constant irritant that keeps us up late and steals our rest. There are only so many hours in a day, only one of us, and only so thin we can stretch ourselves. Taking on more jobs means less time with our children and less time to nurture the one-parent home we are working so hard to make stable and consistent; it is a double-edged sword.

At any given time, you will find me juggling a variety of side gigs. Whether that means accepting last-minute substitute teaching jobs, scheduling content for local organizations' social media, creating digital resources for educators to purchase online, designing websites for Christian ministries, taking on short-term consulting projects, or even DoorDashing — I stay busy finding creative ways to earn. Yes, you read that correctly. My master's degree does not stop me from delivering food! Each opportunity is a chance to learn something new while reaching financial and family goals as a single momma.

To some, this schedule of work might seem scattered, but I see purpose woven through it all. I fully trust that the Lord will provide for my needs, but I also believe He does not call me to sit still. From the beginning of Genesis, He invited humanity into the rhythm of work — not as a burden, but as a blessing. Whether I am designing, teaching, consulting, or delivering, I do it with intention, knowing that meaningful work honors Him.

Though work was our consequence for the first sin of man (see Genesis 3:17–19), in His grace, God blesses His children for laboring. Psalm 128:2 says, "You will eat the fruit of your labor; blessings and prosperity will be yours" (NIV). I like how the New King James Version states, "When you eat the labor of your hands, you shall be happy." What a remarkable promise of future blessings! Our hard work does

> It is a beautiful assurance that our labor, when done with purpose and dedication, leads to future blessings and fulfillment.

not go unnoticed by God. He not only sees our efforts but also blesses us with joy and prosperity as a result. It is a beautiful assurance that our labor, when done with purpose and dedication, leads to future blessings and fulfillment. Theologian John Trapp said it well, "That is, thou shalt reap and receive the sweet of thy sweat, whether it be of the brow or of the brain, according to the kind of thy calling."[5] Though the Lord did not need to bless us due to the sin of Adam, He chose to because of His love for us. What more could we ask for?

God never called us to a rich life, though if we are, is an immense blessing. God called us to a life of peace within Him. With that said, we should work with enthusiasm. God indeed promises His children that He will take care of us, but we must also do our part. God does not just promise to meet our needs, but to provide an abundance. Hard work not only fulfills our needs, it brings more than enough. Idleness reaps insufficiency.

This should bring us great relief as single mommas. God sees the arduous labor that surrounds our daily lives. God sees the backbreaking days where we wake at five in the morning and do not stop till nine in the evening when the children are in their room and settled. God sees the lunch break that is not used to eat lunch but to dash to the local supermarket to pick up snacks for your child's sports team. God sees the tears shed when you look at your bank account and Excel spreadsheet and, despite the hours away from your children to make ends meet, it still will never be enough to own a home or to quickly pay off vehicle debt. God sees you and your daily sacrifice.

> *Even when we feel we have hit an insurmountable challenge, His Spirit has a way of bringing us through our days.*

I more than envied two-parent homes that were bringing in what appeared to be an astounding amount of income compared to my one-parent-home income. The more I compared, the more I was stressed and felt mediocre to my little family. Eventually I was filled with counterfeit guilt on how un-qualified I was to be the leader of my family. Satan is a stealer of joy. Lucky for us single mommas, we have a God-given gift in us that, even when we feel we have hit an insurmountable challenge, His Spirit has a way of bringing us through our days.

So where do we go from here? You desire to see a shift in your finances but have no idea where to even begin—and adding more seems virtually impossible. You want change, but you have a list of doubts. I remember being in this exact place when my daughter started full-time daycare. My minimum payments seemed to do nothing to decrease my graduate-school debt of $35,000, and I was even working full-time at a local university. I was sick and tired of doing my best, and it was not enough for my family.

The next morning on my lunch break, I searched for financial templates on the internet. I found the one that appeared to be the most user-friendly for a beginner, downloaded it, and began to work on recording all my income and main expenses. The file included my weekly salary, child support, therapy appointments, daycare tuition, and college loan payments. Do you know what I noticed? I, shockingly, had money left over.

I wish you could have been there on that lunch break with a half-eaten chicken Caesar salad sitting between me and the keyboard. When I saw the solid black numbers showing that I was indeed on the positive side, my mouth practically dropped to the floor and my hands slapped my desk in awe. I snagged my fork as I threw my hands down onto the desk, and in what appeared to be slow motion, the plastic fork—along with a good chunk of lettuce, parmesan cheese, and chicken—went flying into the air. What a sight to be seen!

That moment was more than a mess on my desk. It was a turning point. It marked the shift from living under the weight of financial stress to taking my first steps toward financial freedom. It may not have looked glamorous, but it was real, hard-earned progress. And it reminded me that sometimes, breakthroughs show up right in the middle of ordinary moments—yes, even during a chaotic lunch break.

But as meaningful as that moment was, I know I am not the only one who needs that kind of breakthrough. Many of us carry silent battles, especially as single mothers, navigating daily responsibilities while looking at the outside of the lives of others. It is all too easy to compare our financial situation to others, and even easier to accept the state we are in. Although it is good to accept our circumstances as a single mother, we should not allow ourselves to accept the stereotypes we hear of single mothers: broken internally and externally. That is a complete lie. We are not financially broke single mommas. We are flourishing Christian mommas.

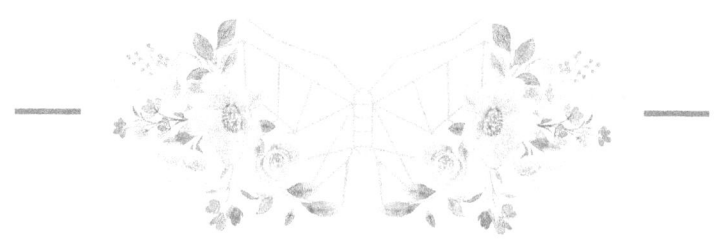

Though it will take much planning and discipline to get where we desire our family to be financially, it is possible. Here are a few practical steps to get you started:

Write down where you would like to see your family. Write a few sentences on where you would like to see your family financially. For example, "I want to save for an emergency fund of $2,000 by the end of the year." Or, "I will pay off credit card debt in the next twelve months." Tape them to your calendar or a place where they can be seen as a reminder to you and your children. It can be hard to say no to in-the-moment joys in favor of long-term freedom, but to be free is well worth it.

Complete a full assessment of current income and expenses. This is one of the hardest parts. You may or may not know where your dollars are going; a full financial assessment will provide you the raw reality of where you are. You may find you are in the black or you may find you are in the red. Either way, you need to know where you are presently so you can get where you desire to go in the future.

Educate yourself on financial freedom. There are a host of books and classes that can aid you in learning about how to get out of debt and build wealth. I recommend any of Dave Ramsey's materials, including his books, website, and Financial Peace University. With these methods, I was able to pay off my $35,000 graduate loans as a single parent, and I know that with a little guidance you can become debt free too! Start off by checking any of his books out from the local library, and once you are able, purchase the books for future reference. Utilize his website and take notes. Many churches offer financial freedom programs for free or a small fee.

Build up a list of hustles. You do not need a degree to bring in income. Think about what you are good at. Could you take on cleaning the home of an elderly family? Do you have a reliable car where you could drive for Uber Eats or Instacart? Perhaps you can take on a part-time job at a local shop or a legitimate online customer support company. Make a list of options to consider and work toward adding one or two that work for you.

Read and repeat. In order to get where you desire to be, you will need to reassess where your dollars are going, review your hustles, and reread your goals, even on a weekly basis. It will keep you accountable and show you where more progress can be made. With your intense focus and determination, you will be shocked where you are in just three months.

Financial freedom as a single momma is possible, but it requires dedication and commitment, especially in the beginning. Paying off debt and building a savings account can often feel like more than just a sacrifice. It may feel exhausting, even discouraging at times. But as you establish healthy financial habits, both in saving and in spending, you will start to see results that speak for themselves. The discipline you practice now will bring lasting rewards, not only in your bank account, but in your sense of peace and stability.

Is it always easy to juggle multiple responsibilities alongside a full-time job? Not at all. There are long days, missed moments, and quiet doubts that try to settle in. But what gives me strength is the reminder that this season is temporary. God sees every bit of the effort you are putting in—the late nights, the sacrifices, the tears, and He is using it all to prepare something greater for you and your family. This journey is not just about financial gain. It is about peace of mind, the ability to rest without worry, and the confidence that comes from stewarding well what God has given you.

Keep pushing forward. Keep going, not just for financial progress, but because you are walking in obedience to what God has called you to in this very moment. He desires for His children to live lives marked by abundance, purpose, and freedom, not just materially, but spiritually and emotionally. When you trust Him with both your work and your rest, He honors that faith.

I cannot wait to see you celebrating, not only the financial milestones, but the growth in your faith and the fruit of His faithfulness. And unlike my lunch, may it be a shower of confetti—evidence of joy and victory, not wilted lettuce! Keep the faith. He is not finished yet.

Prayer

A Prayer for Financial Direction

Gracious Father,

I come to You with gratitude

for the blessings You have given me,

including the financial resources I have.

Help me to be a wise and faithful steward,

using what I have been entrusted

with to support my family,

help others, and further Your kingdom.

Teach me to manage money with

wisdom and generosity, always

remembering that all I have is a gift

from You. May my finances reflect

Your love and purpose.

Amen.

Bible

Scriptures for Financial Peace

*Look at the birds of the air; they do not sow
or reap or store away in barns, and yet your
heavenly Father feeds them. Are you not
much more valuable than they?*
Matthew 6:26

*I know what it is to be in need,
and I know what it is to have plenty.
I have learned the secret of being
content in any and every situation,
whether well fed or hungry,
whether living in plenty or in want.
I can do all this through
him who gives me strength.*
Philippians 4:12-13

*And whatever you do, do it heartily,
as to the Lord and not to men.*
Colossians 3:23

Verses

Scriptures for Financial Peace

*And let the beauty of the Lord
our God be upon us, and establish
the work of our hands for us; yes,
establish the work of our hands.
Psalm 90:17*

*Honor the Lord with your wealth,
with the firstfruits of all your crops;
then your barns will be filled
to overflowing, and your vats
will brim over with new wine.
Proverbs 3:9-10*

*Whatever your hand finds to do,
do it with your might; for there is
no work or device or knowledge
or wisdom in the grave
where you are going.
Ecclesiastes 9:10*

Reclaiming You

Chapter Six
FUELING YOUR PASSIONS

Do you know what my favorite part of the day is? Shower time. I know, it might sound a little strange to call a shower the highlight of my day, but hear me out. There is something undeniably refreshing about it. After a long, grueling workout or hours spent in the heat, nothing beats stepping into a cool shower and washing away the sweat and the lingering warmth of sun. On those rare occasions when I have been bedridden with the flu, barely able to move, a warm bath feels almost miraculous. The simple act of soaking in hot water has a way of resetting both my body and my mind, a much-needed recharge.

On emotionally draining days, there is nothing more comforting than a hot, steamy shower that eases my full self. The steam dissolves the tension in my muscles, softens the weight of my worries, and lifts the mental exhaustion hanging over me.

I have trained my daughter to give me twenty to thirty minutes of quiet during my shower time. Well, to be honest, I did not exactly train her. I just told her, "Unless you are puking or the house is on fire, do not bother me." It is my time and I need it. Not because I am overly concerned with hygiene, but because the shower is the one place where I can quickly reset and recharge. It is a brief escape where I can clear my mind, a small luxury I have carved out for myself. A good high-end soap, a facial mask, and a Bluetooth speaker playing something soothing is how I spoil myself and speedily rejuvenate.

Additionally, what makes the shower truly special is that it is one of the few places in my day where I am completely alone. No one is asking for help. No one is pulling at my attention. No one is interrupting my thoughts. In those moments, it is just me—a true place of solitude in this world. It is the one place where I can shut the world out for a bit, let go of all the responsibilities, and simply exist without needing to be anything for anyone else. These precious moments of calmness help me recharge and reconnect with myself in ways nothing else can.

No matter how tough the day has been, I always feel a little better after I step out of the shower. Every single time, without fail. It is my reset button, my moment of renewal. Yet, despite how much it helps me, how much it refreshes my body and soul, I still sometimes cannot shake the guilt of making time for myself, knowing my daughter is just sitting in front of the television. It is like I am sneaking a moment of selfishness, even though I know a shower is an everyday human necessity.

Even though my rational mind reminds me that those thirty minutes of quiet help me be a better parent, my guilty thoughts push that logic aside. I have been taking long showers for years, just like anyone else, but as a single momma, it somehow feels like a luxury I do not deserve. Every person needs a moment of self-care, so why do we moms feel guilty for taking that time for ourselves? Mom guilt is real.

Over the years though, I have had to continually put effort at stopping that internal mental whirlwind that circulates around and around, making me feel guilty when I drop off my daughter at her grandparents' house so I can take a long hike, get a pedicure, or enjoy an afternoon of coffee with a close friend. I find I feel much less guilty when the circumstance of work or a family emergency requires my daughter to spend time with her grandparents. Did you catch what I did there? Even as I am writing this book and have done the work, I still categorize my personal needs much lower on the totem pole than my job or the family's needs. I guess I have more work to do than I thought.

Do you hold guilt for doing things you love? Do you find it hard to fully enjoy the rare moments you have away from work or your children? Have you tried to take an entire day for yourself, where you planned to take yourself out to eat and do some light shopping, and found yourself back at home doing laundry and scrubbing the shower, something you knew you needed to do for over a week now?

> Dear momma, do you have dried bones? Are you so focused on everyone else's needs that you have forgotten to nourish your own soul?

The internal struggle is real and raw, and it can make self-care feel more like another burden rather than a blessing. Perhaps you went to a movie, but your mind drifted back to your children. Or you could not shake the thought that the money spent on popcorn might have been better put toward your car loan. Instead of enjoying the film, you felt a pang of guilt for being away, for spending money "frivolously," wondering if you should have chosen to stay home with your kids instead.

What if I told you that the Bible actually instructs us to seek moments of joy in our lives for the well-being of our soul? Proverbs 17:22 says, "A merry heart does good, like medicine, but a broken spirit dries the bones." It is not just a poetic proverb to make us feel good. A heart of happiness is essential for our health and well-being; it is medicine to our soul. Without it, we have dried bones.

Dried bones equate to an unhealthy, depleted state, one that lacks life and vitality. We mommas know a thing or two about depletion. There are many times when we have felt stressed out, worn out, and emptied out. It is as if our spirit has been drained to the point where our bones feel dry.

My dear momma, do you have dried bones? Are you so focused on everyone else's needs that you have forgotten to nourish your own soul? It is easy to lose sight of joy when you are constantly giving, but taking moments to nurture a "merry heart" (v. 22) is not only good for your spirit, it is essential for your physical health too. Beyond that, you deserve it.

> He desires for us to enjoy the life we are in, no matter the circumstance.

He desires for us to enjoy the life we are in, no matter the circumstance. Although it can be difficult to accomplish this in the struggle of single motherhood, it is possible to attain. Setting aside unfounded guilt and choosing to enjoy a hobby or quiet time on our own not only makes us better mothers but brings joy to our Lord. When we make space to rest, laugh, create, or simply be still, we are honoring the life He has given us and acknowledging that joy is not only allowed, but encouraged.

God's delight in us is not limited to how productive we are or how perfectly we parent. He takes pleasure in seeing us embrace the moments He has placed before us, even the small ones. Whether it is a walk in the park, a chapter of a favorite book, or a cup of coffee enjoyed in peace, these moments are not trivial. They are sacred. They remind us that God is present not just in the work but in the wonder. Choosing joy, even in a hard season, is a bold declaration of trust in God's goodness.

I am reminded of the song of David that announces grandly, "This is the day the Lord has made; we will rejoice and be glad in it" (Psalm 118:24). David reminds us that God is the Creator of time and everything in it; He has purposefully made each day. The day, with all its challenges and blessings, is under God's sovereignty and control. This day, today, was crafted in detail by our God, a gift for us to fully enjoy. Rejoicing in the present is not always easy, but it is always possible because our joy is not rooted in circumstances but in the One who holds them all.

Theologian Alexander Maclaren reminds us that our deep contentment should not be reserved for the outwardly joyful days, but our spiritual happiness should shine through during the most challenging ones.[6] There is always a reason to find joy each day, embracing the present with a heart full of gladness. Knowing that difficult days are inevitable, do you not think God wants us to do more than just look for the silver lining? He wants us to savor the moments with the people and things we love.

With this in mind, we can choose to "rejoice and be glad"(v. 24) in whatever circumstances we face. Yes, we can choose joy as an act of faith, but we can also take intentional steps toward doing the things that bring us long-term contentment. This balance of faith and action opensthe door to a fuller, richer experience of joy in every season of life.

While I deeply enjoy the rejuvenating experience of long, quiet showers every day, I have also come to appreciate the challenge of long hikes. I make it a point to get outside twice a month for a 10 km hike, and every few months, I take on a half marathon hike. In addition to that, I absolutely love going to the movies, especially when I can catch a film at a theater out of town that has reclining leather seats and cup holders.

When a movie comes out that I am excited to see, I have learned to take advantage of the opportunity by dropping my daughter off to spend some quality time with her cherished grandma and grandpa or hiring a sweet high schooler who does not mind playing dolls and house for a few hours in order to get a reprieve. When she is off to her five-day summer camp, that is my time to catch my next big hike or explore a new city. It is a win for both of us. Consider partnering with another momma in having days that you can switch with for alone time too (more on that in chapter 10).

Carving out time for yourself is necessary for your long term mental and physical health. Think about what brings you solace or energy and is within your budget. Is it a paint by number craft, crocheting, or a long swim? Can this enjoyment be done weekly or monthly? Whatever it is, make it a priority, not a luxury. Even small moments of self-care can make a big difference in your overall well-being, helping you recharge and return to your daily responsibilities of single motherhood with a clearer mind and a lighter heart. You are not being selfish by taking care of yourself. You are being wise. A well cared for mother is better equipped to care for her children.

Maybe you have found yourself thinking, *I have no idea what I actually enjoy.* Momma, I have been there too. It is easy to lose touch with your own passions when you are caught up in the daily demands of being a single momma. You are constantly giving your time, your energy, your attention, and often there is little time left for yourself. The days blur together, and before you know it, your time and energy have been completely poured into everyone but yourself.

It is never too late to rediscover what brings you joy. Sometimes it might take looking for inspiration in mom groups or searching the internet for hobby ideas. Or maybe it starts with simply giving yourself permission to have a few hours to yourself without guilt or pressure. Whatever step you take to reconnect with yourself and add passion to your life is worth the effort because when you nurture who you are, you show up more fully for the ones you love.

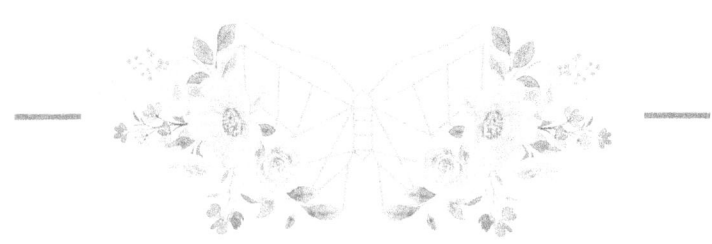

Reconnecting with who you are starts with a little curiosity and a willingness to explore what brings you joy. Be patient with yourself, allowing time and grace as you rediscover your unique self. To help guide you on this journey, here are a few questions to consider:

- What are your current interests, even if they seem small or fleeting?

- Is there a new activity or hobby you have been curious about but have not tried yet?

- What did you enjoy doing as a child or teenager that brought you pure joy?

- What types of things make you lose track of time—in a good way?

- Are there local classes, workshops, events, or meetups that align with your interests?

- What are you naturally good at, or what feels effortless and fulfilling when you do it?

- Could you join a local group, an online community, or a

club to explore those interests with others?

You do not need to justify your need for rest, creativity, or joy. Taking time for yourself is not selfish; it is spirit-lead. When you fill your own cup, you are better equipped to pour into the people and responsibilities you care about. Whether it is a quiet walk in nature, a solo trip to a cozy café, journaling, gardening, crafting, dancing in your kitchen, or getting lost in a good book, these small, intentional moments can refocus you and renew your spirit.

Begin small. Schedule it in, even if it is just for a few minutes each day or an hour each week. Protect that time as you would any other important commitment. You do not need to have all the answers or a perfect plan. Simply begin where you are, with what you have, and trust that God delights in your wholeness.

When you make space for rest and inspiration, you are not stepping away from your responsibilities. You are bringing more joy into your world. When you engage in the things you love, you are not only filling your own cup, but you are honoring the gifts He placed within you. Pursuing what brings you joy is a form of worship, a way to glorify God by living fully and authentically in His purpose for your life.

You were never meant to be lost in the busyness of life. You were created with care, for joy, for rest, and for purpose. You are worthy of this time to rediscover the beautifully gifted, and deeply loved person God made you to be.

Prayer

A Prayer for Enjoyment

Heavenly Father,
I thank You for the beauty and
wonder of Your creation. Help me to
find joy in the simple pleasures of
life that highlight Your glory and
artistry in this world. Open my eyes
to the everyday moments that reflect
Your love—whether in the laughter
of friends or the beauty of nature.
May I embrace these enjoyments
with a heart full of gratitude.
Guide me to seek and celebrate
the things that draw me closer
to You and remind me of
Your goodness.
Amen.

Bible

Scriptures to Guide Your Passion

*I know that there is nothing better
for people than to be happy and to do
good while they live. That each of them
may eat and drink, and find satisfaction
in all their toil—this is the gift of God.*
Ecclesiastes 3:12-13

*A cheerful heart is good medicine,
but a crushed spirit dries up the bones.*
Proverbs 17:22

*Command those who are rich
in this present world not to be arrogant
nor to put their hope in wealth,
which is so uncertain, but to put their
hope in God, who richly provides us with
everything for our enjoyment.*
1 Timothy 6:17

Verses

Scriptures to Guide Your Passion

You are the salt of the earth.
But if the salt loses its saltiness,
how can it be made salty again?
It is no longer good for anything,
except to be thrown out
and trampled underfoot.
Matthew 5:13

You make known to me
the path of life; you will fill me with
joy in your presence, with eternal
pleasures at your right hand.
Psalm 16:11

A person can do nothing better
than to eat and drink and
find satisfaction in their own toil.
This too, I see, is from the hand of God.
Ephesians 2:24

Chapter Seven

Parenting with Intention

"Knees up! Knees up! Let's go!" the trainer on my smart TV urged. Her tight dark curls bounced with effortless rhythm as I struggled to keep pace. The new year had arrived, bringing with it the familiar resolve to eat better and move more. Today, I was determined to power through the 30-minute HIIT workout, but had not planned on the accompanying loud grumbling of my seven-year-old, who could not find her beloved blue and white blanket.

"I will help you when I am done," I huffed.

"Mom, I want my blankie now."

Trying to catch my breath, I said, "I am in the middle of a workout. I will help you when I am done.

"Why can't you stop and just help me now? Mom, I want my blankie now. Can't you be a good mommy and help me?" My heart was already high enough to be in the burning zone, and now it felt like it was going to rip from my chest from her hurtful response.

It took everything in me to control my red face from exploding. "Zoey, go to your room and play with toys. I will help you later!"

"But Mom, I want it done NOW."

I had had it. It did not take much for me to lose control of my temper. The day had already drained me. I had given every ounce of effort and energy to two jobs with different shifts, and all I wanted now was to muster whatever energy was left to get into better shape. In a split second my frustration overwhelmed me. I grabbed the remote, paused the workout, and slammed it onto the floor with a harsh thud. My face burned with anger as I stormed toward my daughter. I stood just inches from her, and the terror in her eyes stopped me cold. They were wide with shock, reflecting the fear of a child staring at a monster who had once been her mother.

"If you do not go to your room right now, you are going to get a massive spanking!" I gritted my teeth so hard that my jaw ached afterward. Her eyes, usually so full of sweetness, filled with tears as she gave me one last terrified glance before running to her room. I stood frozen, staring at the broken remote scattered across the floor, instantly consumed with regret for what I had just done in front of my little girl. Not only had I ruined my work out by smashing the remote, I now stood there paralyzed by guilt as I heard her sobbing alone in her room, scared of her own mother, the only parent she had.

If there is one thing the Bible makes clear about parenting, it is that we are called to parent with intention and diligence. Proverbs 22:6 states plainly, "Start children off on the way they should go, and even when they are old they will not turn from it" (NIV). There is no ambiguity here. The verse does not shy away from the responsibility we, as parents, have. It emphasizes that children need guidance, direction, and intentional training, and that training begins with us. Though a great responsibility, especially for us single mommas, there is a great reward.

How wonderful that if we just do our parental responsibilities, we are blessed. "Even when they are old they will not turn from it" (v. 6). What a beautiful blessing that we and our children will receive; we get to be witnesses of their spiritual growth and steadfastness. When we put effort into parenting our children by teaching them biblical truths while loving them in their growth, we are not just making them great people, we are making them soldiers for Christ, and we as the parent get a front-seat view of it all. We are given a generational blessing, one that continues to bear fruit even when we are long gone. What a gift of grace!

Purposeful parenting is incredibly difficult with two parents, let alone one. I am not even sure *difficult* is the right word, maybe *overwhelming* or *exhausting* would be better. The reality is that the weight of that responsibility can feel unbearable at times, not just occasionally, but *many* times, especially as a single mother. Every decision can feel heavy, and every day can feel like a balancing act between providing for our children, being present for them, and somehow managing the home while trying to find even five minutes for a moment of rest—let alone having the burden of raising spiritually, physically, and mentally strong Christian children on our own.

The pressure to raise them well as a single parent is real. It is up to us to teach them to love God, love others, and love themselves while going through spiritual, mental, and physical growth. I am constantly questioning if I am doing enough or doing it "right." And yet in the midst of all that struggle, there is also the deep knowing that being a parent is indeed worth it. The intentionality, the sacrifices, and the sleepless nights will bear fruit, even if it does not always feel that way in the moment.

If there is one thing in this book that has had the greatest impact on my approach to parenting, it is learning how to manage my emotions with my child, especially my anger. It is not easy to admit that there have been several times when my anger has gotten the best of me. Although my issue with anger has immensely improved over the years, it still can grab hold of me once in a while when my work hours are long and my sleep hours short and my daughter needs attention that my exhausted body just cannot provide. It is then that I remember that grace is given. Now that my daughter is older, I can verbalize that I am exhausted, and she will compassionately hug me and even help me with a few extra household chores. A gift from God, grace goes a long way so we can give it freely to ourselves and our children.

Parenting, at its core, is ninety percent emotion and only ten percent action. The actions we take as parents, the lessons we teach, the rules we set, the routines we establish are important, of course, but it is the emotions given that truly shape our children. It is the love we pour into them, the patience we show when we are exhausted, the empathy we offer when they are struggling, and the trust we build in our relationship with them. These emotional foundations create an environment where children feel safe, valued, and understood. While daily tasks like making meals, helping with homework, or enforcing boundaries are necessary, they are fueled and given meaning by the emotional connection we nurture with intention.

> It is both the difficult emotional moments and the joyful celebratory moments where our children truly see us.

Our emotions are the nucleus of being confident in our management of family life. How we conduct ourselves in any situation is vital to our child's well-being. Our children are not simply completing a multiplication word problem or passively absorbing information. They are watching us in real time; they see us scroll through social media, sometimes distracted or disconnected. They notice when we carry exhaustion on our faces or respond with frustration. They see more than just the surface of our actions; they witness the rawness of our emotional reality. When anger rises as they ask questions in the middle of a workout, or when we hurriedly put together a meal, these moments speak volumes about how we handle stress, love, and patience.

Ultimately, children do not care if the meal we prepare is home-made or if we hold a six-figure job. What matters most is that we show up for them consistently, that we put down our work and give them uninterrupted moments of attention. It is in the difficult emotional moments, the tears, the apologies, the celebrations, that our children truly see us for who we are. It is our reactions, far more than our actions, that guide and shape them. These emotional imprints last long after the day-to-day tasks have faded, forming the foundation of how our children will respond to the world and relationships for years to come.

As we reflect on the immense responsibility and blessing of raising children, we can find comfort and encouragement in God's Word. The psalmist beautifully captures the preciousness of children and the honor bestowed upon parents who choose this calling:

Behold, children are a heritage from the Lord,
The fruit of the womb is a reward.
Like arrows in the hand of a warrior,
So are the children of one's youth.
Happy is the man who has his quiver full of them;
They shall not be ashamed,
But shall speak with their enemies in the gate.
Psalm 127:3–5

King Solomon, rich in money, gold, homes, and even wives, knew that children are a blessing. With blessings comes responsibility. Verse 4 exclaims, "Like arrows in the hand of a warrior, so are the children of one's youth." Like shooting an arrow with a bow, children must be guided with skill and strength. An arrow cannot just be shot without thought if one desires to hit the bullseye. It must be launched with focus and direction right from the start. As parents, we must lean in with confident parenting to lead our children on a solid spiritual path that will direct them to positive choices.

Theologian Charles Spurgeon reminds us, "He gives children, not as a penalty nor as a burden, but as a favour. They are a token for good if men know how to receive them, and educate them. They are 'doubtful blessings' only because we are doubtful persons."[7] Spurgeon points out that children become "doubtful blessings" only when we, as parents, are doubtful or uncertain in our own hearts about our ability to raise them well. When we approach parenting with faith, intention, and wisdom, we begin to see children for what they truly are: blessings entrusted to us.

Parenting does not take perfection. Parent takes prescence.

I know, momma—our children can also feel like a heavy burden, especially since we are on our own managing it all. The food bill, the house constantly dirty, the laundry piling up—it can be incredibly overwhelming. That is all the more reason to pivot to a new path, so that what feels like a burden at times can be seen for what it truly is: overflowing blessings.

Beyond our emotions, improving the way we parent often requires a holistic approach that looks at both our actions and the environment within our households. For starters, it is important to assess if there are things in the home that need to change as we evaluate how we approach parenting. Sometimes it could be as simple as reinforcing a few key rules or setting limits on screen time to create a healthier balance. As parents, we usually know what external changes are necessary to improve the household, whether it is organizing the space better, maintaining consistent routines, or limiting distractions.

Equally important is considering the emotional side of parenting. For example, consistent therapy or setting new expectations for ourselves can be incredibly helpful in managing stress and developing emotional resilience, which ultimately benefits our kids as well.

One of my personal goals, which I discuss in chapter 4, is to set aside dedicated time during the week to have intentional moments with my daughter. Designated time not only gives me a much-needed break from the load of life, but it also provides her with the focused attention she craves after a long day at school.

Additionally, we have developed an "escape plan," a simple strategy either of us can use when emotions start to overwhelm us. Whether it is a breathing exercise, a short walk, or a quick distraction, having a plan in place helps both of us step back, regain control, and reset when things get tense. These small, mindful actions can go a long way in improving both our parenting and the overall atmosphere in our home.

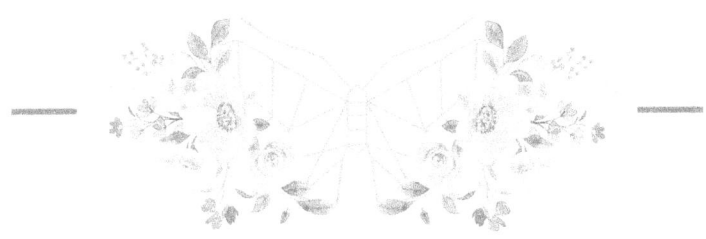

Every family is unique, shaped by the personalities, needs, and rhythms of its members. Because of this, it is important to find routines and practices that feel natural and supportive for your household. What works beautifully for one family might not fit another, so take time to explore and adapt ideas in a way that honors you and your family's dynamic and values. The following suggestions are what has helped strengthen my family's structure, creating more peace at home, and brings us closer together:

Choose Your Family Verse

A family verse is a Bible verse that represents your family's core values and beliefs. It can evolve as your children grow and their needs change. Start by selecting a few verses that resonate deeply with you as a parent and have each child vote on their favorite.

Have each child write the chosen verse on paper and encourage each child to display it in their room with an extra displayed in a shared space, such as the kitchen or living room. The verse can serve as a reminder in both joyful and challenging times, helping everyone remember that your family is united in faith and grounded in Christ.

Choose Your Escape Plan

Every parent has regretted something said in the heat of the moment. It is natural to make mistakes, so it is important to have a strategy to calm yourself and your children during tense times. My daughter and I agreed that when either of us feels like we are about to say something hurtful, we say, "Please give me space right now."

The other person then steps away in silence, waiting for the other to approach when she is ready. This gives us both time to collect our thoughts so that, when we come back together, we can have a calm and constructive conversation about why one of us is upset or frustrated. It works successfully for us, allowing us to go to God first rather than saying something unkind in the moment. What would best work for you and your children?

Assign House Chores

What tasks do your children handle around the house? It may seem easier to do everything yourself, and, well, many times it is. Assigning chores helps teach responsibility and organization. You could create laminated cards listing daily or weekly tasks or jot them down on a calendar. In our home, my daughter has a daily chore list on a whiteboard that she works through when she gets home. As she completes each task, she marks it off with an X.

This visual reminder helps her see what needs to be done in order to earn free time, including time on her iPad. If she does not finish the list, there will be no reason for technology time. While it was tough to establish a routine at first, it is now part of her daily rhythm and keeps her accountable and successful (although the eye rolls are still very present!).

Parenting with intention is about more than setting rules or checking off milestones. It is about cultivating a home filled with love, purpose, and peace—a place where your children feel seen, safe, and deeply valued. It is choosing day by day to create a nurturing environment where their hearts can flourish and their faith can take root. Intentional parenting is not about perfection; it is about presence.

The small, everyday moments are what truly matter. It is the quiet prayers whispered over sleeping children, the gentle corrections offered with grace, the warm hugs that restore confidence, and the words of encouragement that echo in their hearts long after the day is done. These simple acts of love are what leave the deepest imprint. They build trust, create connection, and shape your children's understanding of God's love.

As you move forward, remember that you do not walk this journey alone. With God's help, every choice, every action, and every moment—no matter how ordinary—can be a reflection of His grace. When you feel overwhelmed, God is your strength. When you feel unseen, He is watching over you. When you feel unsure, He is guiding your steps. Trust that He is not only working in your children's lives but also in yours. He is shaping you into the parent He has called you to be, one faithful, intentional, grace-filled step at a time.

Prayer

A Prayer for Parenting

*Heavenly Father,
I come before You seeking
Your wisdom and strength to be
the best parent I can be. Guide me in
nurturing my children with love,
patience, and understanding,
reflecting Your grace in our home.
May my words and actions
encourage their growth in faith
and character, drawing them closer
to You. Fill me with Your Spirit,
so that I can lead them with compassion
and purpose, creating a foundation
rooted in Your love.
Amen.*

Bible

Scriptures for Your Parenting Journey

*My dear brothers and sisters,
take note of this: Everyone should be
quick to listen, slow to speak and
slow to become angry, because
human anger does not produce the
righteousness that God desires.*
James 1:19

*No discipline seems pleasant at the time,
but painful. Later on, however, it produces
a harvest of righteousness
and peace for those who have
been trained by it.*
Hebrews 12:11

*Discipline your children,
and they will give you peace;
they will bring you the delights you desire.*
Proverbs 29:17

Verses

Scriptures for Your Parenting Journey

*Love the Lord your God
with all your heart and with all
your soul and with all your strength.
These commandments that I give
you today are to be on your hearts.
Impress them on your children.
Talk about them when you sit
at home and when you walk
along the road, when you lie
down and when you get up.
Deuteronomy 6:5-7*

*All your children shall be
taught by the Lord,
And great shall be the
peace of your children.
Isaiah 54:17*

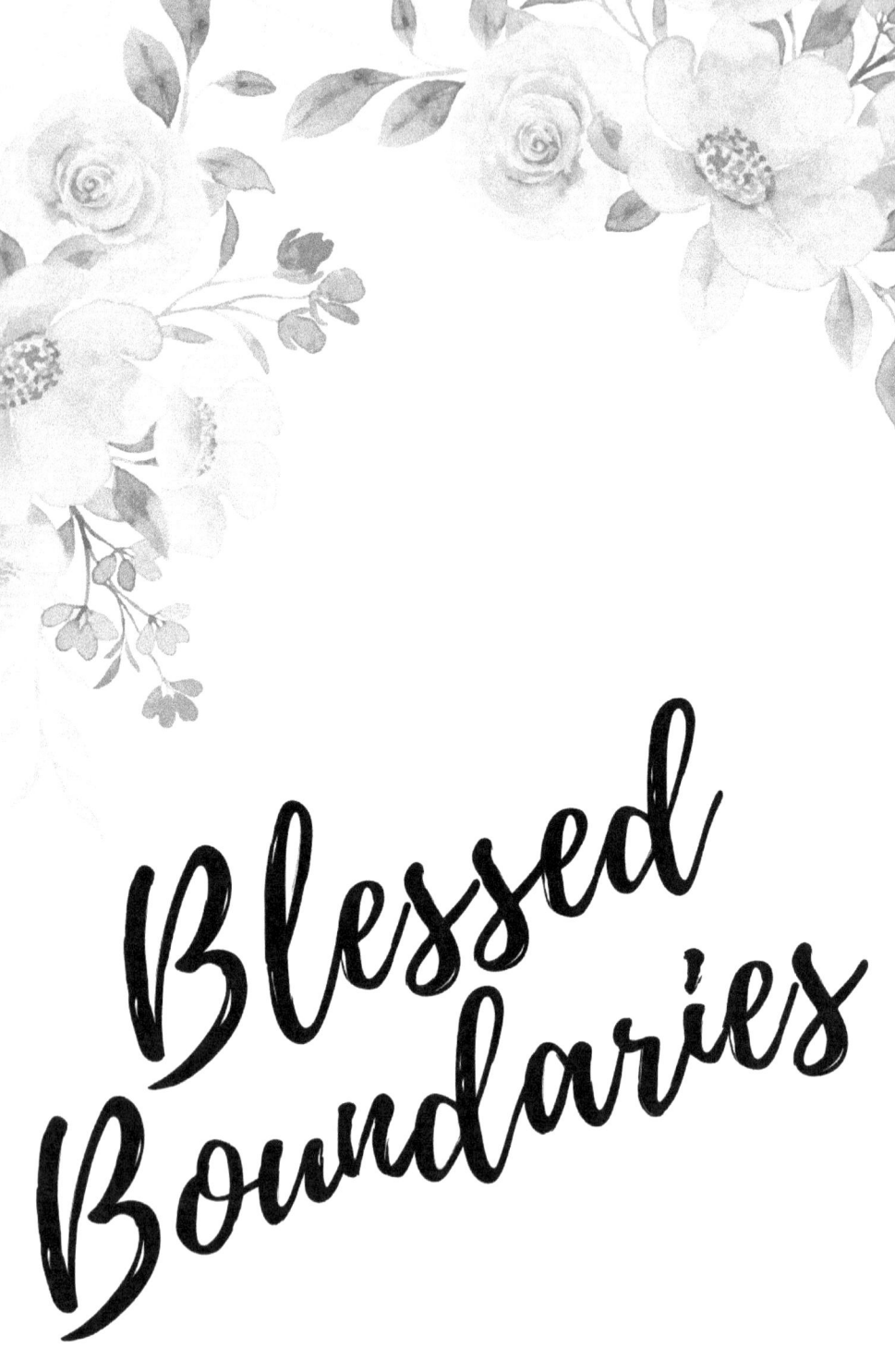

Blessed Boundaries

Chapter Eight
THE OTHER PARENT

Buzzz. Buzzz. Buzzz.

The vibrating hum of my iPhone on the wooden kitchen table made my heart drop. Despite the silence around me, the notification felt like a loud, deafening presence, sending a rush of adrenaline through my veins. I hesitated, the weight of anxious anticipation thick in the air, holding me captive just a moment longer.

Oh, that sound from the iPhone can bring so many reactions. From my mother, the musical vibration can cause me to smile from her sweet message. From my friend, a chuckle at a mom joke about our erratic pubescent children or happiness at an invitation to coffee. From my sister, a shaking head caused by reading about my young nephew being his funny self. From my ex-husband, well, ultimate dread overcomes me.

I spend the next twenty minutes making up lists in my head that I can complete in lieu of going to my phone. Alas, it must be done. I stammer my way to the kitchen, encouraging my apprehension by picking up shoes left by my ten-year-old. *Perhaps it is not from him. I bet it is my friend texting me to let me know about our next get-together.* My uneasiness loosens at the thought but is quickly tightened when I pick up my phone to see his name on the screen.

Buzzz. Buzzz. Buzzz. Another notification alerts me of another email from him. I close my eyes in hopes it may aid me in calming my spirit.

Buzzz. Buzzz. Buzzz. And another one. Nope, my spirit is not serene.

The continual email messages, though short, are many times too much to bear. His accusations of my ill parenting are endless, even though he has not seen this beautiful child in years. *Here we go, the message war begins.* If I do reply, it does not matter what I write; it always ends badly. His words are like arrows, sharp and piercing, even when they carry no truth. Though email is the only method he is allowed to use to reach out (due to his inability to control his tongue), the interaction still is not what it should be. It should be a way to share updates and to bridge the distance between father and daughter. Instead, it is a battleground. Oh, how I long to open an email that asks how my beautiful little girl is doing or what is happening in her life, but it rarely, if ever, turns out that way. They are not questions of care or genuine interest. They are disguised attacks, riddled with blame and self-righteousness, his way of still attempting to wield power from over five hundred miles away.

Though it has been over ten years since I fled his house with nothing more than a few bags, terrified of what he might do next, narcissism still looms like a dark cloud before a heavy storm in all communication. I thought the distance (and time) would fade the bitterness, but it has not. Every email feels like another reminder of the person I escaped and how that person is still somehow haunting my present. He may not be physically in our lives anymore, but his words that drudge up flashbacks are little more than a click away.

Have you ever been there with your child's other parent? A simple text message, a quick exchange of words, and suddenly everything feels like it is on the edge of exploding. The smallest miscommunication quickly spirals into a full-blown confrontation, each word laced with accusations that sting, leaving your emotions raw. Even when you try with every ounce of your being to stay composed, the weight of their explosive explanations, the ones that insist you are not a good parent, easily overtake you. It is as if they have found a way to reach inside and tug at your deepest insecurities. A short phone call about something as mundane as your son's dental bills will turn into an attack on your character, as if you are only after his money. It happens so fast, so unexpectedly, that you are left reeling, struggling to catch your breath and keep the situation from unraveling further in your present.

Before you even know it, a routine drop-off at their dad's house becomes a battleground. What was meant to be a quick exchange of custody turns into a verbal altercation in front of the kids. And just like that, your resolve to follow your mom's advice of "If you have nothing nice to say, don't say anything at all" is tossed out the window. It is like you have no choice but to defend yourself, even though you know it is not the right approach. You want to be the bigger person, to take the high road, but it is so hard when you feel like your every effort is being minimized, your every word twisted. You are doing your best, but somehow, it feels like that is never enough. He makes it impossible to stay calm, and you wonder how you can keep moving forward without letting it all consume you.

It is incredibly easy to give into deception and incredibly difficult to choose discipline. It is not easy when the other person is purposely making decisions or speaking words to get back at you, rather than what is in the best interest of your children. Every word or action feels personal. And well, it is. It is personal because your role as a mother is the most important job you will ever have.

Mind you, it is not easy, whatsoever. As single mommas we are quick to defend because we work so very hard at being two-parents-in-one in our household. We desire affirmation, even from our previous relationship. In the end, it may never matter what we do or what we say; nothing will change the other parent's opinion of us. We cannot control their thoughts or feelings, but we can control ours and what we do with them in our present.

Trusting in Him allows us to rise above the chaos and respond with patience and clarity.

Over recent years, I have clung to Psalm 119:68 as a prayer of surrender when interacting with my ex-husband or with anyone with whom I find it difficult to communicate. The verse has become a way for me to calm my spirit in tense situations, helping me shift my perspective. Instead of viewing these moments as conflicts, I see them as opportunities to worship and trust God. In my mind, I repeat, "You are good, and what you do is good; teach me your decrees" (Psalm 119:68 NIV). Trusting in Him allows me to rise above the chaos and respond not from frustration, but with patience, clarity, and peace.

The author of the psalm did not allow his emotions to take control. Instead, he looked to God for a better perspective and deeper wisdom. He understood that in times of difficulty or confusion, we can always trust in God's inherent goodness and always seek His guidance. In the midst of his own circumstances, he affirmed that God's actions are always with purpose and aligned with His love for us. Moreover, despite affliction, the psalmist chose to have discipline and depend on his heavenly Father for direction.

The writer specifically asked, "Teach me your decrees" (v. 68), knowing that with wisdom and guidance, he could make better decisions. He trusted that whatever he faced was part of God's best plan for him, and rather than dwelling in negative feelings that could hinder him, he chose to trust that God ultimately was what was best. With a little dedication, we, too, can do the same.

I still struggle in this area, especially when my ex-husband accuses me of being a bad mother. I know my mouth has gotten me into a world of trouble. It can be extremely challenging to be the bigger person and control my tongue when I feel under attack. Proverbs 21:23 reminds us that, "Whoever guards his mouth and tongue keeps his soul from troubles." What we say profoundly impacts our spirit. When we respond wrongly, even if the other person is attacking wrongly, our soul will not be at spiritual rest. Similarly, when we choose to speak rightly, or perhaps to not speak at all, our soul will be at peace, even during difficult conversations.

What we say profoundly impacts our spirit.

We must choose to be cautious and deliberate about what we say and how we respond if we truly desire peace within. It is incredibly difficult to refrain from saying what we truly think, but choosing our words carefully and avoiding impulsive reactions is exactly what we need to do to receive the peace that comes from God. Although difficult, controlling our tongue is 100 percent worth peace within ourselves and our children.

Many times, it does not feel fair that it is up to us to be the better person. Remember, it is not for the other person. We guard what we say because we are believing mommas who love the Lord and love our children and we know that we have God to fight for us and protect us. Commentary of Proverbs 21 reminds us, "Yet much prayer and forbearance are required to avoid being upset by every trifle. This will keep us from being irritated needlessly. We must also bear in mind that we have divine support for all our heavy crosses. We also look forward with intense longing for the home of everlasting peace."[8] When we choose the higher ground, we can be confident in His love for us and in His purpose for our family.

How can you improve interaction with the other parent? What needs to be done in order for you to come out on the other side of an interaction feeling confident that your actions displayed God's best as a believer? Perhaps it is repeating Psalm 119:68 over and over in your mind or putting it in your car and reading it before pickup or drop-off. Maybe it is something entirely different, such as utilizing a co-parenting texting app where you can have time to read and respond to messages in a godly way. Remember, this is not for the other person. It is for you—protecting your heart, mind, and soul.

With God's guidance, co-parenting can become an opportunity to model grace, unity, and love—even in challenging circumstances. By keeping your focus on what is best for your child while leaning on your faith, you can turn even the most difficult situations into opportunities for personal and spiritual growth. Here are some suggestions for improving co-parenting and fostering a healthier, more collaborative relationship.

Keep to a Parenting Plan

Sticking to a clear parenting plan and court order is essential in co-parenting because it ensures that both parents are on the same page regarding boundaries, responsibilities, and expectations. Consistency in following these agreements helps minimize confusion and conflict, creating a more stable environment for the children.

Communicate Effectively

What tools can be utilized to decrease friction or confusion? Using a parenting app or an online shared calendar can be a great way for co-parents to stay organized and communicate effectively. Any tool that will allow you to easily track schedules, appointments, and important events will reduce the chance of miscommunication or double-booking.

Stay Kid-Focused

Keep communication child-focused when talking with your co-parent to ensure that discussions remain productive and centered on the well-being of your children. If the conversation is not about the child, consider a blanket statement to pivot the conversation. It may be better not to respond at all.

Delay Response

If the conversation about the children feels sensitive, try setting a timer for fifteen minutes before responding. This gives you time to pause and to avoid reacting impulsively with harsh words, allowing you to reply more God-thoughtfully and wisely. When emotions are high, refrain from even texting at all and wait till a phone conversation can happen with both parties are at ease.

Small moves add up to big ones, especially when it comes to navigating the complexities of co-parenting. Setting clear boundaries is essential. It creates a foundation of respect and structure that both parties can rely on.

By doing your part, whether it is sticking to the parenting plan or maintaining consistent communication, you contribute to a more stable and predictable environment for your children, even if your co-parent does not. Your consistency can become a source of comfort and grounding for your child amid uncertainty.

At the same time, it is important to release the things that are beyond your control—whether it is the actions of the other parent or unexpected challenges that arise. When emotions are running high and you feel overwhelmed, turn to God for harmony and guidance. He is your ultimate source of strength, offering wisdom to navigate the hard moments and grace to keep your heart steady. By letting go and leaning on God, you create space for peace, healing, and a clearer path forward.

Prayer

A Prayer for You and Your Children

Dear Lord,
I ask for Your help in becoming
a person who honors You in all that I do.
Fill my heart with kindness and
integrity, and guide my actions
so they reflect Your love and grace.
I also lift up my children to You,
praying that they grow in faith and wisdom.
Surround them with Your protection and
lead them on paths of righteousness.
Thank You for the privilege of being their
parent; help me to nurture them
with Your truth.
Amen.

Bible

Scriptures for Godly Character

I have set the Lord always before me;
Because He is at my right hand
I shall not be moved. Therefore my
heart is glad, and my glory rejoices;
My flesh also will rest in hope.
Psalm 16:5-9

If it is possible, as far as it depends on you,
live at peace with everyone.
Romans 12:18

I have set the Lord always before me;
Because He is at my right hand
I shall not be moved.
Therefore my heart is glad,
and my glory rejoices;
My flesh also will rest in hope.
Psalm 16:8-9

Verses

Scriptures for Godly Character

Create in me a pure heart, O God,
and renew a steadfast spirit within me.
Romans 51:10

And He said to me,
"My grace is sufficient for you, for My
strength is made perfect in weakness."
Therefore most gladly I will rather boast
in my infirmities, that the power of Christ
may rest upon me. Therefore I take pleasure
in infirmities, in reproaches, in needs, in
persecutions, in distresses, for Christ's sake.
For when I am weak, then I am strong.
2 Corinthians 12:9-10

For the Spirit God gave us
does not make us timid, but gives
us power, love and self-discipline.
2 Timothy 1:7

Moving On

Chapter Nine
To Date or Not to Date

My daughter has been asking for a "real bed" for a while now. Her black loft bed was a lot of fun when she was younger, but now that she is a tween, and almost as tall as I am, she has grown tired of bumping her head on the ceiling and climbing up and down at night for a drink of water.

I vividly remember when I proudly put together that high loft bed all by myself five years ago, piece by piece, screw by screw. One would be shocked at how I held up the sides and attached them without any help. But today, here I was, standing in her room, utterly exhausted and stuck in the corner against the wall, desperately trying to hold up two sides of that same loft bed. I did not think taking it apart would be so much more difficult.

What once seemed like an impressive feat now felt like an insurmountable task. Struggling to disassemble the bed, it became clear that taking it apart was far harder than putting it together ever was. The parts were heavier than I remembered and refused to cooperate, as if everything were working against me. My arms ached, patience wore thin, and the colossal pieces seemed impossible to manage alone. Suddenly, the pieces tumbled, pinning me in the corner of the room. I yell out to my daughter for help.

She came running, and despite being almost as tall as I am now, her strength and youthful energy did not offer much in terms of holding up the heavy metal frame. She tried her best, yet it was clear this was not something I could do alone. The weight of the bed seemed to press down on both of us, and as I stood there, struggling to keep everything together, an overwhelming wave of frustration and sadness washed over me.

Suddenly, I could not hold it in anymore. "This is not fair," I cried out. "It is just me! There is no one here to help me. No man here to fix it. I cannot do this!" A wave of tears followed as I physically broke down. I sobbed under the bed frame, upset that I had voiced my desire for a male figure in the home—something I had never mentioned to my daughter before—and been overwhelmed by the loneliness I felt in that moment. I have always tried to keep a strong front, especially in front of her, yet in that instant, all my frustrations, exhaustion, emotions—and the weight of everything—seemed to pour out at once. I cried harder than I had allowed myself to in a long time.

Managing things without a man around had often been a point of pride for me. The household bills were managed well by me. I was the sole driver on every single one of our road trips, even the 15-hour trip to Omaha. The picnic table had been relocated and rotated to different areas on my patio multiple times. Assembling a ridiculous 95-piece children's kitchen set had been a particular achievement for me. After that, I felt unstoppable!

But that pride, that sense of accomplishment in doing things on my own, never fully covered the moments when I needed help, when I was reminded of my limitations and of how much I could not do alone. There were days I needed a male friend to come over to change a stubborn light bulb or to check my Toyota when the engine belt was giving me trouble or to help me hook up the washer and dryer.

Even with all my independence, those were the moments when I longed for more, when I wished for someone to rely on, not just for practical help, but also for emotional support. I wished for someone who could be my forever partner, someone to share the burden with, someone who would step in and say, "I've got you." In those quiet moments, the weight of it all would settle in, and I could not help feeling the ache of loneliness. Have you had those moments too?

There are times when the house feels a little too quiet, a little too empty. The kids are at their extracurricular activities or spending the weekend with their biological father, and suddenly, the stillness of the house becomes more glaring. That 25-piece IKEA shelf, neatly packed in its box, sits there glaring at us, an unwelcome reminder that we just are not the greatest at these kinds of puzzles.

We know it is something we will just have to figure out on our own, but the thought of spending the next few hours bent over instructions, wrestling with tiny screws and pieces that do not quite fit, feels like one more task in a long line of jobs that we need to accomplish on our own. In those lonely moments, the silence makes the weight of those solo responsibilities feel heavier than usual. It is in those moments that the desire for a husband sounds loudly over it all.

And then there is the toilet. Just when we think everything is under control, one of the kids innocently, or perhaps not so innocently, flushes a bouncy ball down the toilet during their bedtime routine. The water starts to rise, and we find ourselves in damage control mode again. Or you wake up cold, only to learn that your water heater hit the fritz. It is moments like these, the unexpected messes and the small crises that seem to pop up at the most inconvenient times, that remind us how much we wish there was someone else to share the load with. Someone to step in without hesitation, to make the chaos feel a little less overwhelming.

And then there is the toilet. Just when we think everything is under control, one of the kids innocently, or perhaps not so innocently, flushes a bouncy ball down the toilet during their bedtime routine. The water starts to rise, and we find ourselves in damage control mode again. Or you wake up cold, only to learn that your water heater hit the fritz. It is moments like these, the unexpected messes and the small crises that seem to pop up at the most inconvenient times, that remind us how much we wish there was someone else to share the load with.

We all desire to be loved.

Even when your comfy couch is full of pillows and blankets, the couch feels empty at night once the kids have gone to bed. The space between the cushions seems wider, the silence deeper. In those moments, you realize how much you long for more than just help.

You long for true companionship, for authentic partnership. You long for someone to be there, not just to fill the space, but to share in the challenges, the laughter, and the quiet moments of the day. You want someone who understands your struggles without needing an explanation, someone who celebrates your victories, no matter how small, and who simply enjoys being present with you. You want to have someone to lean on, to make the burdens feel a little less heavy. You want to find comfort in shared responsibility. To have someone to truly be with you. We all desire to be loved.

Let me echo: *We all desire to be loved.*

Yet as Christian single mommas, there is a stereotype that we should not date. That in fact, we should refrain from dating until our children are older or until we are older. Many believe that pursuing a relationship while managing being a single parent would be selfish or irresponsible. Even those who know us well may discourage us from taking on another "responsibility." This well-meaning advice, which many have shared with me kindly, has made me feel guilt or shame that I do not deserve. Have you heard similar comments as well?

"God loves you. Focus on Him right now."

"You are doing great on your own!"

"Don't remarry. You don't need a man."

"Your child comes first now. Do not risk hurting her more."

"Just focus on your cutie pie, and maybe after she graduates someone can come along."

And, of course, my favorite: "God is your husband."

The "encouragement" some gave me about dating as a single momma was quite unenjoyable. Though many of these comments were said with a sincere desire to uplift, they often felt more like reminders of my "failure"—as if my broken marriage disqualified me from wanting love again. Rather than bringing comfort, their words sometimes served as a subtle punishment for a divorce I never wanted in the first place. It felt as though I was being told to settle into a lifetime of solitude, as though love, intimacy, and companionship were no longer meant for me.

"God is your husband," many have told me. While I may not have rolled my eyes physically, my mind was swirling with frustration. This phrase is taken from Isaiah 54:5, which says, "For your Maker is your husband, the Lord of hosts is His name; and your Redeemer is the Holy One of Israel; He is called the God of the whole earth" (NKJV). Unfortunately, this verse has been misused countless times. It was never intended to shame or limit a woman's desire for relationship. The author uses the relationship between a husband (God) and wife (Israel) to illustrate how God will redeem Israel. Though Israel may feel abandoned like a widow, God promises to stand in for them. It is a metaphor of hope and restoration, not a command for single women to forgo a relationship.

Without a doubt, God is with you and me to comfort and strengthen us. He is indeed our Maker and our Redeemer. God will meet *all* our needs in this world. And in a way, God is our husband because no man, or any human, can really provide us unconditional love like God can. A commentary I read stated, "An earthly husband can never fulfill every need that the great Heavenly Husband can."[9] Many have forgotten that the verse applies to everyone and was not written solely for the single mother, but for all. Our pure desires to have a mate are still very much present and natural.

> *A worthy walk allows us to not only find a mate who is worthy of our time and efforts but also ensures our children are positively impacted by this person.*

Though there are not any verses in the Bible that talk about specifically dating, let alone dating as a single momma with children, we do have a number of verses in the Bible that speak on the qualities of a godly husband and wife. I encourage you to read through these with commentary, digging deeply into what to look for in a mate. Write down these biblical qualities and refer to them continually as you search for a partner, if that is what you desire at this moment.

Understanding these qualities can help clarify what truly matters in a relationship. Proverbs 20:7 states, "The righteous man walks in his integrity; his children are blessed after him" (NKJV). A true man or woman of God will ensure that their faith walk can be easily seen in their actions. When he or she acts in faith, their children are blessed for it.

If we choose to date, we should do our best to make sure that both the person we are dating and ourselves are walking in faith. A worthy walk allows us to not only find a mate who is worthy of our time and efforts but also ensures our children are positively impacted by this person.

"If you were to date right now, would this man of God feel that he has found 'a good thing?'" This difficult question was asked of me by a dear friend. Without a doubt, I can still feel the sting today as I did on that day. Sometimes truth can hurt, even from a loving friend. She was correct. Though I desired to date, to try to catch the dream of a beautiful and godly two-parent home that I felt was stolen from me, I was nowhere ready to date.

Proverbs 18:22 is clear in that, "He who finds a wife finds a good thing and obtains favor from the Lord" (NKJV). We desire to have a loving and supportive relationship and to be blessed by that relationship. However, our healing can significantly influence the strength and godliness of a potential partnership, either fostering growth or creating unneeded challenges.

Therefore, healing becomes a foundational part of our journey. Our healing journey as a single momma plays a vital part in the success of a future marriage. Dating is already a daunting task, but if we are not spiritually and mentally in a Holy Spirit filled place, we may miss red flags or ruin a relationship that could flourish in the long term. If we want to see success in our dating, it is important that we focus on working on ourselves first so that when we meet the person God has for us, we will be a blessing to our partner.

When we cultivate a strong relationship with God and nurture our own emotional health, we build a foundation that can support a healthy, lasting relationship. Remember, the right person will not complete you, they will complement the fullness of who God is shaping you to be.

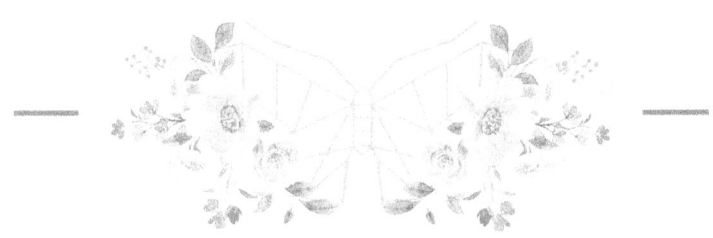

Self-awareness is a key part of growth, and asking the right questions can help illuminate what is beneath the surface. Reflect on each of these questions on in order to gain a deeper understanding and perspective of where you are.

- Where do you currently stand in your healing journey from past relationships?

- What aspects of your current circumstances might support or challenge the possibility of a healthy, godly relationship?

- Considering your child or children's stage of development, do you feel this is a good time to pursue dating?

- How would you describe the current emotional and physical well-being of you and your children?

- Are you genuinely open to or actively seeking a relationship at this point in your life?

A few steps that can be taken to set you up for dating success:

- Make a list of nonnegotiable standards that outline what you are looking for in a partner. A list of ten or so qualities that are clear and concise, and also biblically based, will allow you to see your preferences more clearly.

- Think about what your dating boundaries are with communication. We live in a world that is all technology, and many times it is difficult to see red flags through text.

- Look at your dating boundaries with physical touch. Just because you have been physical with a man in the past does not mean you cannot choose to abstain now. We are held to timeless biblical standards.

- Consider the timing of introducing someone to your children and how it might impact them, both positively and negatively.

Deciding to date is a deeply personal choice—one that should be made with prayer, reflection, and an honest look at your current reality and readiness. There is no "one-size-fits-all" answer. Depending on your circumstances and where you are in the healing process, you may feel that now is the right time or that it is better to wait. Either choice is valid when it is led by wisdom and the Holy Spirit.

Although the idea of a man being there by my side to help me put together or take down a 65-piece loft bed sounds like a dream come true, having the wrong man in that place can ultimately tear apart an entire family. A relationship that is not aligned with God's plan has the potential to hurt not only you but your children as well. Protecting the gift of peace and your household must always come before romantic convenience.

At the same time, there is tremendous blessing in choosing singleness—especially when it is a decision made with purpose. (1 Corinthians 7 speaks beautifully to this.) Singleness offers a sacred space to deepen your relationship with God, explore your identity in Christ, and pursue healing and growth without distraction. It allows us to focus on our children with clarity and pour our energy into building a Christ-filed home rooted in peace, love, and stability.

Whether you feel called to remain single for a season or step prayerfully into the possibility of dating, remember this: God is faithful in every chapter. May we continue to seek His will above all else, trusting that His plans for us are always good—whether we walk this journey solo or hand-in-hand with someone else.

Prayer

A Prayer for Your Relationships

Dear God,

I come to You seeking guidance

in my relationships. Help me to

trust Your will, knowing You know

what's best for me. Whether or not

I have a partner, may I find my worth and

fulfillment in Your love alone.

Give me wisdom, patience, and

discernment to make choices that

honor You and lead me to relationships

aligned with Your purpose. Let me

walk in Your peace, trusting

You are in control.

Amen.

Bible

Scriptures for Relationships

*Delight yourself also in the Lord,
and He shall give you the
desires of your heart.
Psalm 37:4*

*Do not be unequally yoked
together with unbelievers.
For what fellowship has
righteousness with lawlessness?
And what communion
has light with darkness?
2 Corinthians 6:14*

*But seek first the kingdom of God
and His righteousness, and all
these things shall be added to you.
Matthew 6:33*

Verses

Scriptures for Relationships

Love suffers long and is kind;
love does not envy;
love does not parade itself,
is not puffed up; does not behave rudely,
does not seek its own, is not provoked,
thinks no evil; does not rejoice in iniquity,
but rejoices in the truth; bears all things,
believes all things, hopes all things,
endures all things.
1Corinthians 13:4-7

Above all else, guard your heart,
for everything you do flows from it.
Proverbs 4:23 NIV

Do not be deceived:
"Evil company corrupts good habits."
1 Corinthians 15:33

Momma Tribe

Chapter Ten

CULTIVATING COMMUNITY

If there is one part of being a single momma that I am successful at, it is being on my own practically. To this day, I pride and thrive on being a one-woman show. Time and time again, people tell me, "Melissa, I do not know how you do it. You are like superwoman!" Those words always bring a smile to my face, like a badge of honor, affirming that my single motherhood journey has not gone unnoticed. Oh, it feels so good for people to see me fly solo.

Juggling multiple jobs, providing for my daughter's every need, keeping the house running smoothly—all of it became my modus operandi. It was not just about surviving the daily grind; it was about thriving in it. My superpower? I flourish in the chaos.

Well . . . on the outside at least.

Externally, it always appeared I was crushing single motherhood. I loved boasting about working three part-time jobs so that I can make my nonprofit organization that serves people in Kenya a priority. Of course, I can make sure my kid is on the honor roll and participates in the school musical while I write a book or two. Getting up at 1:30 in the morning to have a team meeting with people in Kenya and still being at my next job by 7:30? Easy peasy. I have the gift of flourishing in chaos and showing the world that, despite my circumstance of single motherhood, I am a force to be reckoned with. However, this appearance of a strong front is a major weakness in reality.

Rather than being truly proud of my progress, many days ended with me alone in tears, angry that I had to do it all on my own. In these times, I realized I was nothing like my façade as a super-woman. Rather than contentment, I felt I was empty with nothing else to give. Tired—completely and profoundly tired. Every effort, every small victory felt hollow, as though it was just another item checked off a never-ending list. I had given so much of myself, too much, and in return, all I had was an overwhelming emptiness, like I had poured my energy into a bottomless well.

The constant demand for more, from both myself and others, weighed on me in ways I could no longer ignore. It felt like no matter how much I did, it was never enough. I could see the expectations in others' eyes, always reaching for something further, something bigger, but I had nothing left to give.

Some days, I wondered how I ended up here, this person who is supposed to have it all together who is only barely holding it all in place. And I realized: I have been playing this role for so long that I forgot how to take care of the one person who needed me most, myself.

I am not sure when I became the person who could do everything for everyone else and refuse anything that brought me joy. Even now, I am lost in the silence of my own exhaustion, longing for a moment of rest, a chance to breathe, a reason to smile without pretending. Deep down, I know why I am where I am.

Doing it all on my own was what I prided myself on because I did not want others to see my "weakness." Do not get me wrong, working multiple jobs is necessary for me, at least in this stage of my life, and I am indeed proud of my daughter's school success, yet when the sun sets and the moon appears, I am completely alone. I did not want others to help me because it reminded me that I was indeed on my own, without a husband and a father for my daughter. I did not want others to feel obligated to fill in the apparent holes in my one-parent household. No matter the outward success, that loneliness still permeated it all.

Solitude can be a sanctuary, but it can also feel overwhelmingly piercing. In the deep silence of our alone time, our minds and hearts often wander, bringing to the surface the harsh realities of being a single mother. While navigating life alone may feel familiar, it is the daily solitude that can ignite a fiery anger in our hearts—anger that's hard to soothe. There are times when the weight of responsibility becomes so heavy that silence is no longer peaceful, but suffocating, with each passing second serving as a reminder of what we carry by ourselves. There are moments when the weight of responsibility presses so heavily that the silence is not tranquil, but rather suffocating, each second a reminder of what we carry alone. In the quiet, we replay the struggles, the missed opportunities for help, and the endless sacrifices we make without a second thought.

The truth is we do not just carry the physical load of raising children on our own, we carry the emotional burden of wondering if anyone sees us, if anyone understands how much we are doing just to survive each twenty-four hours. The silence amplifies that isolation, making us question our strength, our work, and even our choices. It is easy to feel invisible when every day is a battle to balance work, parenting, and our own sense of self. And as much as we love our children, there are days when the absence of adult conversation or support makes life feel like an echo of what we once dreamed of.

There are many reasons why we may or may not have a tribe to lean on. For some of us, the absence of a support system comes from the weight of single motherhood guilt. The thought of accepting help, whether for ourselves or our children, can feel shameful. There is embarrassment in needing assistance because of a broken relationship, shame in knowing we cannot always give back what we have been given, and indignity in admitting that, despite our strength, we are not invincible or self-sufficient.

For some of us, it is a matter of pride. There is something empowering about being 100 percent independent, about proving to the world (and ourselves) that we can handle it all. It feels good to say we do not need anyone, that we can thrive without anyone else's help. We can play the role of the superwoman who does it all alone—well, until the exhaustion hits and we realize we have drained ourselves dry, exhausting all our energy.

And then there are those of us who have simply learned not to trust. At one time, we trusted someone completely, someone we thought would be there forever, someone who was supposed to be our best friend, our support. When that trust was broken, the idea of relying on anyone again became unthinkable. We make a promise to ourselves that we will never let anyone get that close again. Or maybe, when we have reached out for support in the past, our need has been met with excuses or empty promises with no follow-through. After a few failed attempts to put ourselves out there, it is easy to give up.

For me, it was a mixture of all the above. I feel guilty when asking anyone for help, and I always feel I need to return the favor. Pride feels good when you have convinced others that you are unbreakable. I have lost trust in people due to past failed relationships with my spouse and others. Sometimes it feels easier to be on my own.

But the reality is that you cannot do it on your own long term. Why? Because it was not how God designed us to live. "As iron sharpens iron, so one person sharpens another" (Proverbs 27:17

NIV). We were created for the community, to encourage and grow together. While personal devotion time, like those quiet moments early in the morning, is essential for our spiritual growth, interaction with fellow believers is just as imperative. We need godly friends to walk alongside us, especially in the unexpected journey of single motherhood.

It is not just about us. It is about the mutual support we offer one another. Our friends, whether they are single mommas or not, also benefit from the encouragement and strength we share. One of the lessons I missed for a long time in Proverbs 27:17 is that both pieces of iron are sharpened, not just one. In a truly reciprocal relationship, you are not the only one receiving. As much as you are refined by the

You cannot do it on your own long term. Why? Because it was not how God designed us to live.

company of others, they are shaped by you too. The beauty of having a tribe, a community of strong women, is that it is not one-sided. You pour into others and they pour into you. There is a shared strength that comes from walking together, helping each other grow, and providing a support system that nourishes both parties. In this way, both you and those in your tribe are sharpened, strengthened, and equipped to face whatever challenges come your way.

Two-parent home, one-and-a-half parent home, one-parent home, every parent needs support whether it is childcare coverage for an early dismissal, parenting advice on a tween entering puberty, or figuring out a dentist bill. All these events are the same, no matter the homelife. In other words, a tribe is just as needed when on our own as it would be if we had a spouse. There are so many benefits to committing to a community.

> *There is a shared strength that comes from walking together, helping each other grow.*

King Solomon reminds us, "Perfume and incense bring joy to the heart, and the pleasantness of a friend springs from their heartfelt advice" (Proverbs 27:9 NIV). As theologian Waltke explains, "The gladdening oil and incense is a simile for the agreeable and delightful counsel of a friend that originates in his very being. Both the outward fragrances and the wholesome counsel produce a sense of wellbeing."[10]

While external comforts, like perfume and oil, can indeed brighten our day, it is the counsel of a friend that can provide true nourishment to our soul. A friend's advice, delivered with care and grounded in truth, becomes a source of refreshment that touches the very core of our being. It is this kind of friendship that brings true joy and stability, offering us not just momentary relief but continued support on the path of peace.

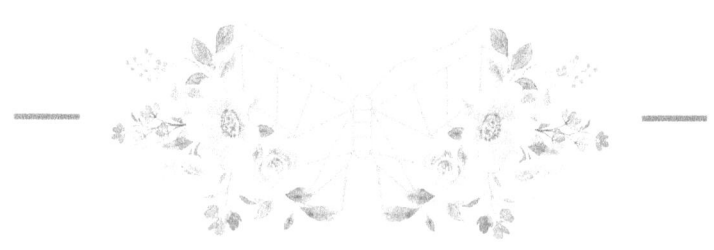

What steps can you take to connect with others? Even without close family nearby, there are still numerous ways to connect with others. Consider joining a women's Bible study where you can bond with like-minded women who share your faith and values. Local gym classes or fitness groups can also provide opportunities to meet others while helping you maintain your physical and mental health. Social media is another great tool. Many online groups and pages specifically cater to Christian single mothers, offering advice, encouragement, and connection. Additionally, look around for fellow moms in your circle who might be open to a "trade day" arrangement where you swap childcare responsibilities for a day. Let us work through a few key steps to help you build your community:

Take Inventory: Make a small list of people in your family and community who you currently connect with. Think about friends, acquaintances, or even church members who are open to lending a hand or offering emotional support. Reflect on who you can potentially add to the list.

Join Groups: Search for groups that align with your situation and needs. Whether it is a single mom's group, Celebrate Recovery, or an online mom's support group. These groups provide emotional support, practical advice, and shared experiences that can help you navigate the challenges of single motherhood.

Say Yes: Decide to say yes the next time a family member or friend offers to take your kids for an afternoon. Say yes without shame or fear. Often, we feel hesitant to accept help, worrying about burdening others or feeling guilty for taking time for ourselves. Saying yes with confidence to an offer of help is an important step toward building a supportive community.

Supportive community might look like a friend who texts just to check in, a mentor who speaks truth into your life with love, or a sister in Christ who prays for you when you do not have the words. It might be someone who notices when you are struggling and offers a kind word or an encouraging reminder that you are not alone.

It can also look like someone who brings over dinner, watches your kids for an hour, or just sits on your couch and listens. These seemingly small acts carry immense power—they remind us of

God's love made visible through others. In those quiet, generous moments, we experience the beauty of being held up by the body of Christ. Sometimes, it is not about fixing anything—it is just about being there.

Your willingness to build and receive community also teaches your children the value of vulnerability, connection, and faith-filled relationships. You are modeling what it looks like to live with open hands and an open heart, and that is a legacy with eternal significance.

So be brave. Take the first step, even if it feels awkward. Open the door, send the message, show up. Let God use others to strengthen you and trust that He will also use your life as a blessing to those around you.

Prayer

A Prayer of Support

Dear Lord,

I seek Your guidance in being a

source of support and encouragement

to those around me. I also pray for

Your provision in bringing grounded, Jesus-

filled people into my life,

forming a community that reflects

Your grace and truth. Lead me

to those who will walk alongside

me on this journey, so together we

can glorify You and support

one another in our lives.

Amen.

Bible

Scriptures About Fellowship

Carry each other's burdens,
and in this way you will
fulfill the law of Christ.
Galatians 6:2

Every day they continued to meet
together in the temple courts.
They broke bread in their homes
and ate together with glad and sincere
hearts, praising God and enjoying
the favor of all the people. And the Lord
added to their number daily those
who were being saved.
Acts 2:46-47

As iron sharpens iron,
So a man sharpens the
countenance of his friend.
Proverbs 27:17

Verses

Scriptures About Fellowship

*And let us consider one another
in order to stir up love and good works,
not forsaking the assembling of ourselves
together, as is the manner of some,
but exhorting one another, and so much
the more as you see the Day approaching.*
Hebrews 10:24-25

*For as we have many members
in one body, but all the members
do not have the same function,
so we, being many, are one
body in Christ, and individually
members of one another.*
Romans 12:4-5

*How good and pleasant it is when
God's people live together in unity!*
Psalm 133:1

Soul Repair

Chapter Eleven

MENDING THE SOUL

As a busy single mom, I often find myself struggling to stay mentally clear and emotionally balanced in the present moment. Perhaps I am in the middle of a work meeting or doing laundry, and in a flash, an old memory suddenly resurfaces in my head. It takes but a few seconds for my eyes to start watering as I allow myself to stop and my heart to reminisce.

Like the oversized stocking, full of the colors and designs of Christmas, that I found stuffed between my daughter's winter clothes as I was unpacking from storage. The Christmas stocking looks as new as the day I purchased it over a decade ago when my ten-year-old was newly born. And in fact, though technically old, it has still never been hung, ever. The name "Dad" knitted so perfectly along the very top of the jovial stocking, screaming to be hung on Christmas Day. The reminder of that first beautiful Christmas for a mom, dad, and babe that never was still produces a deep ache after all these years.

I could easily throw that Christmas stocking away, and perhaps I should, yet my heart would equate that to throwing away a dream. Yet another dream, yet another desire, yet another future plan that I feel I was forced to abandon since becoming a single momma. Tossing the stocking away means me accepting that I will never remarry, that I will always be alone. Despite all the pain, the tears, and the unfairness of becoming a single mother, that oversized stocking reminds me of hope. Hope that one day I will be blessed with a godly man who will honorably accept the name of Dad for my daughter. Hope that one day I can experience what it is like to spend Christmas with someone who will not only be there on Christmas Day but be there for all the memory-making holidays. Hope that one day this stocking will be used. So much emotion from one old, yet unused, Christmas stocking.

Do you have moments like that too? Moments when you are crushing single motherhood by finishing up that massive load of laundry, or cleaning out the packed closet, or paying all the bills on time, and then suddenly you come across an item that brings back an old thought, an old memory, an old dream. In just a few short moments you find yourself with watery eyes of sadness, or a red face of anger, or a frown of disappointment as you reminisce.

The healing process is especially long for single mothers because it is incredibly difficult to heal when there is no opportunity to stop the busyness, both physically and mentally. Many times, we do not have the luxury of taking a few days off from work or going on a solo trip over the weekend to reflect and reset. We cannot take an afternoon for some therapeutic shopping or spend an entire day on the couch binge-watching our favorite reality show. Therapy might fit in once in a while, but the cost often keeps us from doing it more. We might buy a self-help book but never fully read through it—maybe even this one you are holding. Our lives as single moms simply do not offer the time we need to heal completely.

Additionally, many of us find ourselves in situations where we must communicate with our former partner to arrange child pickups or overnight stays. These interactions are mentally draining and often feel like a tug-of-war. Each exchange can reopen old wounds and stir unresolved issues, prolonging the healing process and, at times, leaving us feeling like emotional recovery is an elusive dream.

How are you holding up, momma? Are there days, maybe even good days, that still leave you feeling mentally drained because of flashbacks or internal conversations with your difficult past? Maybe you have decided to begin dating again and the dates are beyond disappointing, causing you to think the failure of these potential relationships means there is something wrong with you. Maybe finances are still incredibly stressful for you or, despite your immensely good financial status, you are still wondering what is next. It often seems like you take four steps forward and then four steps back, keeping you in the same mental space, just with more time passed.

There really does not feel like there is enough time for us to breathe, let alone to heal. But through our healing, we can become better mothers, more effective providers, improved communicators, and better in every aspect of our lives. When Jesus mends our brokenness, we also begin to feel whole again with a lifted heart. His healing gives us the strength to face challenges with renewed hope and purpose. As we heal, we not only transform our own hearts, but we leave space for new hopes, new dreams, and new memories.

King David also experienced healed brokenness. He wrote a heartfelt confession to God after his grave sin with Bathsheba. In the psalm, he lays bare his brokenness and seeks restoration: "Create in me a pure heart, O God, and renew a steadfast spirit within me" (Psalm 51:10 NIV). David makes two significant requests to God: a "pure heart" (v. 10) and a "steadfast spirit" (v. 10). His plea goes beyond forgiveness, seeking a profound transformation and a complete renewal of himself. David understood that true restoration was not about simply wiping the slate clean. It was about receiving a brand-new heart, one that was fully aligned with God's will.

Who else can renew hearts but God? David knew that only the Creator Himself could perform such a deep and lasting work in his life. This is a powerful reminder for us today as well. Just as David turned to God for the transformation of his heart, we too can only find true renewal in Him. No amount of self-effort or external change can give us a new heart. It is only God who can create in us a pure heart and a steadfast spirit, restoring us to the people He designed us to be.

> We cannot experience a transformed heart without also having a transformed spirit.

We cannot experience a transformed heart without also having a transformed spirit. The two go hand in hand, working together in the process of true renewal. One cannot be fully changed without the other being surrendered. King David, who was a powerful ruler and one of the wealthiest kings of his time, understood this intimately. Despite all his wealth, status, and influence, he recognized that his healing and restoration could not come from any external source. True transformation required a posture of humility before God.

David knew that in order to truly experience God's help and healing, he had to rely on God fully, and that meant humbling himself completely. He cried out for an unshakable spirit, asking for God to renew him inwardly so that his soul would be rooted and secure in the Lord. He understood that only through inner transformation could he stand strong against temptation and walk in lasting obedience. His prayer reminds us that strength of spirit is not self-made. It is Spirit given.

Likewise, we need that unwavering, Holy Spirit led heart to guide us on our journey to healing. It is not enough to simply seek mental restoration. We need a heart grounded in God's truth and a spirit anchored in His strength. A sincere heart is essential, but it cannot endure the battles of life on its own. Without a spirit devoted to the Lord, our efforts will eventually wear thin. It is only through His presence within us that we find a steady path, one that can silence the lies of the enemy and protect us from spiritual discouragement.

When we face the challenges of life, those moments when we feel tossed by circumstances, fear, or doubt, it is that deeply rooted faith in God's promises that holds us steady. This kind of spiritual resilience is not built overnight; it is formed through daily dependence on the Lord. Just as David cried out for a renewed heart and a steadfast spirit to withstand temptation, we too must continually invite God to transform us from the inside out. He alone can equip us with the strength to persevere, stand firm, and walk forward in healing.

Let us take a moment right now to invite God to search our hearts, to reveal any areas where we might be holding on too tightly or not trusting fully. It is a chance to ask Him to create a pure heart and a renewed spirit within us. When we make space for God to move in our hearts, we open ourselves to His guidance and grace. So let us approach this moment with humility and openness, asking for clarity, healing, and direction, trusting that God will meet us exactly where we are. When finished, let us read a little more about what the Word says about our hearts.

As we reflect on inviting God to examine our hearts, it is important to also consider the wisdom found in Scripture about the heart's role in our lives. Another king, King Solomon, offers wise counsel to his sons about the importance of protecting the heart. He advises, "Above all else, guard your heart, for everything you do flows from it" (Proverbs 4:23 NIV). Solomon emphasizes that the heart is not just a seat of emotion, but the very core of who we are. Together with our mind, the heart shapes and influences every part of our lives. It is the hub from which our thoughts, feelings, decisions, and actions all flow, driving the direction we take in life and impacting the quality of our relationships.

> We must be vigilant and intentional about guarding what we allow into our hearts and what flows out of them.

It is tempting to react defensively toward your children's father or to belittle your own feelings when a date does not go as expected. However, this verse reminds us to safeguard our hearts, allowing it to serve as a source of wisdom and strength. When hurtful words or troubling thoughts arise, our hearts can protect us by guiding us with insight and discernment.

The New King James Version puts it best: "Keep your heart with all diligence, for out of it spring the issues of life" (Proverbs 4:23). This shows that guarding our hearts requires effort on our part, especially since the enemy constantly provides opportunities to hinder our healing and distract us from God's plan. Therefore, we must be intentional and diligent in protecting our hearts, making conscious choices to nurture what brings peace, joy, and restoration.

The heart encompasses much more than just emotions. It is a reflection of our inner being, our values, and our deepest desires. Our choices, whether big or small, are influenced by the condition of our heart.

If we allow our hearts to be filled with the fruits of the Spirit—love, joy, peace, patience, kindness, goodness, faithfulness, gentleness, and self-control—our actions will naturally reflect those qualities (see Galatians 5:22–23). On the other hand, if our hearts are filled with bitterness, fear, or self-serving emotions, those traits will inevitably flow out in the way we interact with others and approach life's challenges.

Therefore, we must be vigilant and intentional about guarding what we allow into our hearts and what flows out of them. Cultivating a heart rooted in God's love and truth will shape not only our healing but also our relationships and overall well-being.

Working through the contents of your heart and mind, especially when addressing past trauma, can be a daunting and overwhelming task to undertake alone. While walking with Jesus is the foundation of your healing journey, it is also wise to consider other avenues of support. Consider the following:

- Reach out to Christian counselor who can provide valuable guidance and tools for healing.

- Reading faith-based books focused on the healing journey.

- Connecting with a fellow Christian single mother who can be a listening ear.

- Attending support groups like DivorceCare or Celebrate Recovery.

- Journaling your thoughts and feelings as a way to process emotions.

If you are looking for encouragement on the emotional and mental journey of single motherhood, be sure to check out *Unwaver-*

ing Peace: Finding Rest as a Single Momma with a Limitless Jesus by yours truly. This resource dives deeper into the inner healing process—offering hope, honesty, and Christ-centered guidance for navigating the mental and emotional weight that often comes with this season. Because healing is not just about surviving; it is about thriving from the inside out.

———————————————

Embracing the journey of healing not only transforms us individually, but also creates a ripple effect for those around us, especially our children. When we move forward with compassion and grace, we model strength, faith, and resilience. Healing empowers us to become the best versions of ourselves, equipped for the life God has called us to live. And in that transformation, we create space for a brighter, healthier, and more joy-filled future for both ourselves and our families.

Prayer

A Prayer for Healing

Dear Lord,
I come to You in my brokenness,
seeking healing and ultimate peace
in Your presence. Help me to embrace this
journey, understanding that my struggles
can lead me closer to You.
Grant me the wisdom to learn from
my pain and to trust in Your perfect
plan for my life. May each step I take
toward healing deepen my faith
and reliance on You, bringing me comfort
in Your love. Thank You for Your
unfailing support as I seek to grow
in my relationship with You.
Amen.

Bible

Scriptures for Restoration

He heals the brokenhearted
and binds up their wounds.
Psalms 147:3

Then they cried to the Lord in their trouble,
and he saved them from their distress.
He sent out his word and
healed them; he rescued them from
the grave. Let them give thanks to the
Lord for his unfailing love and
his wonderful deeds for mankind.
Psalms 107:19-21

Praise the LORD, my soul,
and forget not all his benefits -
who forgives all your sins and heals
all your diseases, who redeems your life
from the pit and crowns you
with love and compassion.
Psalms 103:2-4

Verses

Scriptures for Restoration

*The Lord is close to the
brokenhearted and saves those
who are crushed in spirit.
Psalm 34:28 NIV*

*Come to Me, all you who labor
and are heavy laden, and I will give you rest.
Take My yoke upon you and learn from Me,
for I am gentle and lowly in heart,
and you will find rest for your souls.
For My yoke is easy and My burden is light.
Matthew 11:28-30*

*Heal me, Lord,
and I will be healed;
save me and I will be saved,
for you are the one I praise.
Jeremiah 17:14*

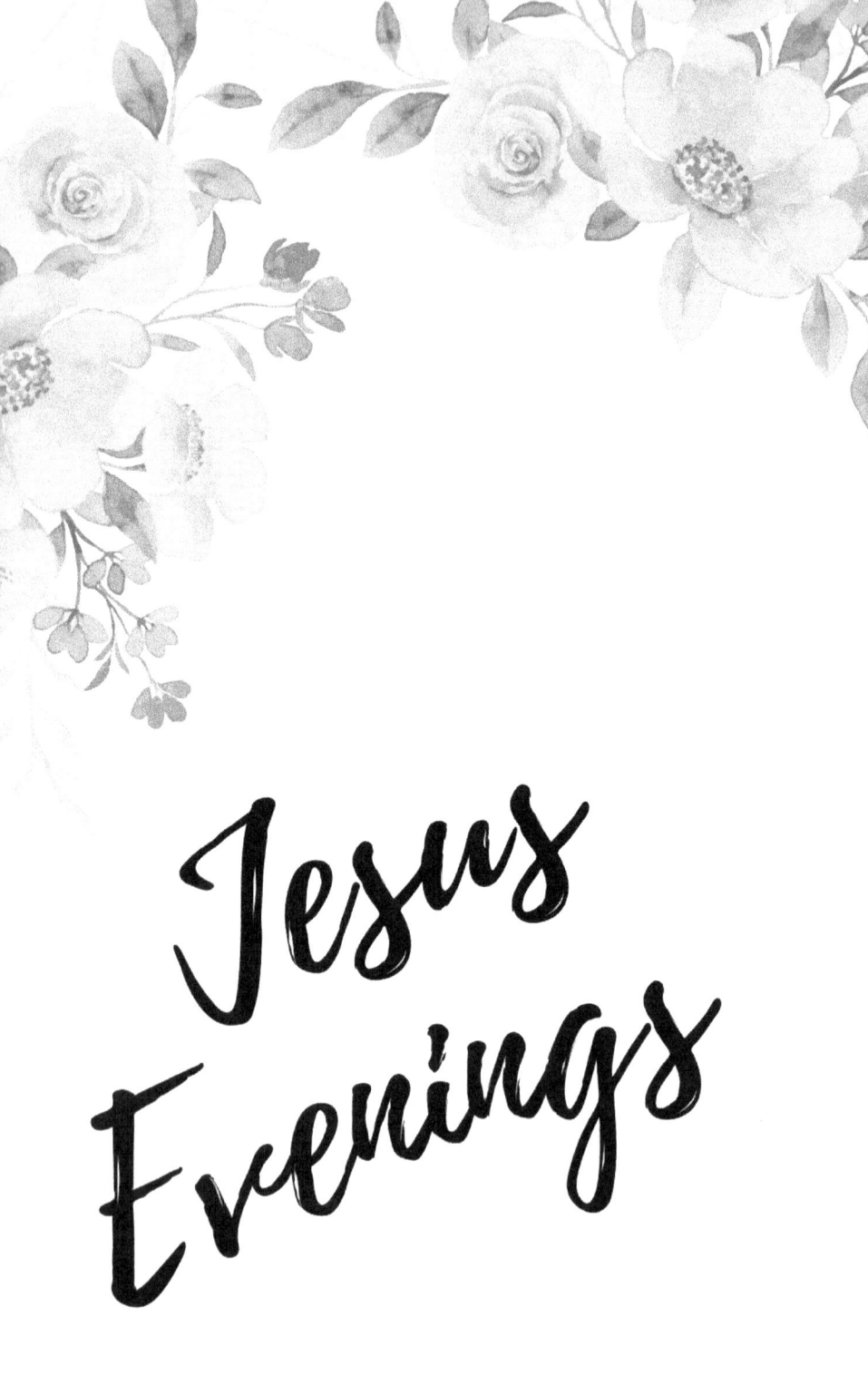

Jesus Evenings

Chapter Twelve
MEETING JESUS AT MIDNIGHT

Here we are. We have made it through another chaotic week. The kids are tucked away in their beds, peacefully sleeping. Well, except our teenager who does not think we know he is playing his Switch. Although the laundry is not perfectly folded and put away in drawers, at least it is all clean in baskets on the bedroom floor. The dishwasher is in rinse mode and trash is in the garage, ready for Monday pickup.

We want—no—we deserve a few hours of downtime with Netflix running in the background so we can shop online on the iPad while munching a big ol' piece of cold pizza. The two delectable buttercream sugar cookies from the local bakery will be our ultimate reward.

Over the past few years, I have deepened my relationship with God by putting Him first. Literally, first. When my morning alarm goes off, the very first thing I do is walk to my makeshift office—that is really a small walk-in closet—switch on a bronze lamp, and open the Word. Okay, mommas, many times I do run to the toilet first. You and I both know we mommas cannot hold it that long!

At first, I had to be intentional in setting an alarm to make sure I spent ten minutes in the morning with Him, whether it was reading, praying, or listening to worship songs. As I dedicated time specifically for Him, I found myself falling in love with Jesus all over again. Now I set an alarm during my Bible study, not because I need to make sure I spend enough time with Him, but because once I start diving into Scripture with commentary, time flies by so quickly that I risk being late to one of my many responsibilities. Even if I only spend fifteen minutes in His Word, it sets the tone for my entire day. This morning routine has become a habit; but the evening, well, that is a different story.

But you see, as a single mother, I have given my entire day to others. Aside from the few quiet minutes I carve out with Jesus in the morning, every other moment belongs to someone else. The early hours are spent helping my daughter prepare for school—packing her lunch, making her a small breakfast, signing that last-minute permission slip. Then, once she's out the door, my focus shifts to the organization I founded, which works to bring the same resources and opportunities we have in the States to communities in Kenya. Add in a few side hustles to support my family financially, and the day quickly becomes a blur of responsibilities.

By the time the school bus brings my daughter home in the afternoon, I switch gears again—homework help, 4-H obligations, church activities, and any number of other commitments that pop up. It is a full, nonstop life. Eventually, she heads to bed, and although I am completely exhausted, I still crave a few minutes to myself—time that is not about productivity or service, but simply about being.

I thoroughly enjoy those quiet late-night moments, drifting off to sleep on my comfy couch, surrounded by fluffy pillows and wrapped in an ultra-soft faux fur blanket. My guilty pleasure? Reality TV. The drama is oddly comforting after a day of constant movement. But truthfully, it is not the best setup for a peaceful night's rest. More than once, I have found my dreams hijacked by the chaos on screen—scenes of wild heists or being chased by an FBI agent playing out in vivid detail. Rest, it seems, is still something I'm learning how to claim.

If you are anything like me, interacting with anyone seems un-interesting after a tiring day, and frankly, I become extremely lazy (and all too self-serving) to dedicate a few moments of the evening to the Lord. Though I know continual time of detachment is an unhealthy way to cope with the woes of tomorrow, in the moment, it feels like exactly what I need and deserve as a single momma who made it through the day. Though a temporary enjoyment, ending the day with gunshots rather than a few mo-ments with our Savior will not bring long-term joy.

Setting a nightly Jesus-time routine has been one of the biggest spiritual game changers of my life, though it was the most dif-ficult to incorporate. Once I established the routine, both my mind and heart were taken aback by the changes. Spiritually, I grew deeper with God through another time of devotion with Him—yet in a unique way. I found that I slept better and, when I awoke, the first thing in my mind was not something I forgot to do the previous day or any disagreement I had had with a friend. It was a worship music lyric unconsciously playing in my head or a whispered *Thank You, Jesus, for this sleep.* I woke up with my body more rested. The morning alarm was not as much of a torment.

It can happen for you just as it did for me and for King David, who testified, "The cords of the wicked have bound me, but I have not forgotten Your law. At midnight I will rise to give thanks to You, because of Your righteous judgments" (Psalm 119:61–62 NKJV). Yes, David's sleep was still interrupted, but not by worry or fear. Instead, it was a divine wake-up call. In those moments, when everything else is still, God often speaks in a way we cannot ignore. David did not see his sleepless night as a burden but as an opportunity to draw closer to the Lord.

> Even in the stillness of the night, we can choose to turn our attention to god, lifting our hearts and hands in prayerful worship.

And how did David respond to the late-night wakefulness? He rose. What a glorious way to be woken—in the presence of the Lord! Instead of rolling around in his bed attempting to sleep, which I am sure he did as much as we do, David chose to rise from his bed to pray and praise. It is a powerful reminder that sometimes our sleepless moments are invitations to connect with God in ways we might miss during the busy day. In many of our modern-day churches, prayer is often associated with kneeling and clasped hands, while praise is usually linked with standing and raising hands. In the Old Testament, however, the posture for both prayer and praise were often the same: hands raised and looking up to God.

For David, when he was woken in the middle of the night, he did not just lie there with anxiety or frustration. He chose to rise, whether to pray or to praise, to glorify God. This choice reflects a heart that longs to worship regardless of circumstances. David's response shows us that even in the stillness of the night, we can choose to turn our attention to God, lifting our hearts and hands in prayerful worship. Whether it is in times of distress or in moments of unexpected wakefulness, like David, we can rise in prayer and praise to honor the One who sustains us. This simple, yet powerful act of rising in praise invites God into our most vulnerable moments and transforms them into opportunities for spiritual renewal.

I am not saying for you to experience God you need to wake up at midnight and stand up in the darkness with hands raised, looking up to our beloved Savior . . . but why not? Rather than roll around in your bed for hours on end, unable to sleep, make it a habit to get up, look up, and praise up in the darkness. Rather than the last sound we hear being a scene from a rerun, why not our favorite worship song. Rather than spending our last moments awake and in worry, why not quietly reflect on a Bible verse or our Jesus-filled statement we made in chapter 1.

Every evening, my daughter and I recite the Bible verse below as a prayer, often adding our specific requests afterward. There are times, even after prayer and evening quiet time alone, that my heart still feels too much a part of a draining world. I will spend time lying in bed breathing, taking deep, long breaths and repeating these prayerful, beautiful words by King David: "In peace I will lie down and sleep, for you alone, Lord, make me dwell in safety" (Psalm 4:8 NIV).

David found ultimate rest in sleep because he recognized that true peace comes from the Lord, not from his external circumstances or his ever-changing emotions throughout the day. Despite facing trials, enemies, and turbulent situations, David's calmness in the Spirit did not depend on the chaos around him or the unpredictable nature of life. Instead, it was rooted in his understanding that peace was not something he could manufacture on his own; it was a divine gift that could only be found in God's presence.

David's ability to rest was deeply intertwined with his trust in God's sovereignty. He knew that true safety and serenity were found in God's protection, not in the temporary comforts of the world. No matter the threats or uncertainties, he could lie down with confidence, knowing that the Lord was his shield. For David, peace was not the absence of trouble but the presence of God's unwavering care and power. It was a stillness that transcended circumstances, allowing him to find rest even in the midst of his most challenging seasons.

Peace is not the absence of trouble but the presence of God's unwavering care and power.

Like David, we can experience profound peace in God's presence, even during times of distress. Instead of lying awake, tossing and turning, consumed by worry or the words of others, we can choose to rest in the unshakable truths of God's Word. When we align our hearts and minds with His promises, we allow His harmony to guard our thoughts and our rest. As a result, not only do we experience emotional and spiritual serenity, we also find that it leads to better physical rest, rejuvenating us for the day ahead.

Spending time with God each night, even if it is just for a few moments, can transform your sense of peace and perspective. This intentional time of stillness allows you to release the weight of the day, invite spiritual rest into your heart, and welcome His guidance through the night. Whether it is a moment of gratitude, a simple prayer, or just being still before the Lord, these few moments of connection can set the tone for restful sleep and a deeper trust in God's presence.

Make the decision to spend time in the evening with Jesus. It does not require hours of your time or elaborate rituals—sometimes, the simplest moments are the most impactful. Even just a few quiet minutes can make a significant difference in your evening. Taking time to pause and connect with Him allows you to reset your heart and mind, releasing the stress and worries of the day. Whether through prayer, reading Scripture, or simply sitting in His presence, these moments help you refocus on what truly matters and ground you in His peace. In a world that constantly pulls for your attention, these small but intentional pauses help center your heart and mind on His unshakable truth.

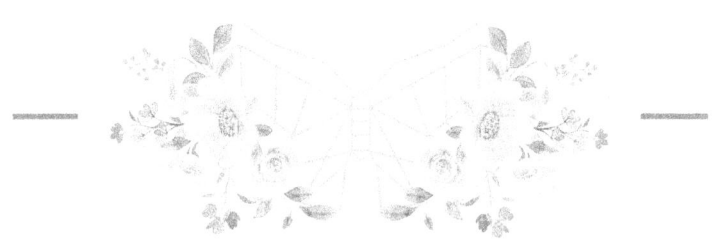

Intentional time with Jesus before resting brings peace and prepares you to sleep with a sense of calm and trust, knowing that you are in His care. It is like placing your burdens down at His feet, allowing His love and grace to envelop you as you rest. Here are a few suggestions:

- Buy a 365-day evening devotional book for nightly reflection.

- Use the Bible app for a brief devotional or prayer time.

- Listen to worship music, allowing God to speak to your heart through song.

- Read the "Verse of the Day" from your favorite Bible website or app.

- Open your Bible and point to a verse, then meditate on its meaning.

- Begin a gratitude journal to reflect on and acknowledge God's blessings in your life.

- Spend time in silence, being still and listening for God's voice in the quiet moments.

As you make this time with Jesus a regular part of your evening routine, you will notice a shift in your heart and mind. Even in the busyness of life, these quiet moments with Him can be a refuge, offering the kind of rest that only He can give. Let Him be the one who restores and refreshes you, night after night, preparing you for the day ahead.

———————————

Let God's truth soak deeply into your heart and soul, allowing it to transform the way you think, feel, and live. His Word is not just words on a page; it is alive and powerful, capable of nourishing you from the inside out. When you intentionally take time to absorb His promises and wisdom, you begin to experience a renewal of mind and spirit that shapes every part of your life. This transformation is not always instant, but with patience and faith, it grows steadily, guiding you toward greater peace and clarity.

There is nothing the Lord desires more than to spend time with you. He longs for a personal relationship where you open your heart fully to His love and guidance. In those quiet moments of connection, when you pause to listen and be still, you will feel His presence surround you. It is in this sacred space that His peace floods your soul, and the assurance of His nearness fills you with confidence. God is always ready to speak, lead, and walk alongside you in every area of your life, offering comfort and strength for the journey ahead.

Prayer

A Prayer for the Night

*Gracious Lord,
as the day comes to a close,
I seek Your guidance and peace in the
quiet of the evening. Help me to unwind
and release the burdens of the day,
filling my heart with gratitude for
Your blessings. I ask for Your
protection and comfort as I prepare
for sleep, that my mind may be
calm and my spirit at rest. May
I find solace in Your presence,
allowing me to wake refreshed and
renewed for the day ahead.
May I trust in You as I surrender
to a peaceful night's sleep.
Amen.*

Bible

Scriptures for Peaceful Nights

Evening, morning and noon I cry out
in distress, and he hears my voice.
Psalm 55:17

One of those days Jesus went out to a
mountainside to pray, and spent
the night praying to God.
Luke 6:12

About midnight Paul and Silas
were praying and singing hymns to God,
and the other prisoners were
listening to them.
Acts 16:25

My eyes stay open through
the watches of the night, that I
may meditate on your promises.
Psalm 119:148

Verses

Scriptures for Peaceful Nights

*Evening, morning and noon I cry out
in distress, and he hears my voice.
Psalm 55:17*

*One of those days Jesus went out to
a mountainside to pray, and spent
the night praying to God.
Luke 6:12*

*About midnight Paul and Silas
were praying and singing hymns to God,
and the other prisoners were
listening to them.
Acts 16:25*

*My eyes stay open through
the watches of the night, that I may
meditate on your promises.
Psalm 119:148*

Conclusion

As I write this conclusion after an incredibly long and challenging day—fourteen and a half hours of work across three different jobs—I am surprised that I managed to make dinner from a box and still carve out time for nightly devotions with my little girl. The light in my bathroom has been out for a week now, and I have grown accustomed to showering blindly. Our dryer has turned into an impromptu dresser drawer, and the kitchen table has become a catchall for softball, school, and a 4-H sewing project. There is nothing profound to showcase externally, but internally, I feel a profound sense of peace.

Though mornings arrive too quickly and too early, the stillness of the morning fills my heart and home. Amid the daily chaos, I am certain that God has a specific purpose and plan for me, for my daughter, and for us together as a small family. The calendar may be full, yet it remains manageable. The work hours can be long, but if an emergency arises, I am financially prepared. The harsh emails from my ex still come, yet I have set clear boundaries. By evening, I am exhausted, but I choose to open my Bible and look up to Him, falling asleep knowing that God holds it all in His hands. I can surrender it all to Him.

Momma, the same is offered to you. Though uncertainty is part of our single motherhood journey, we are strong and deeply loved by the One who created the universe. As believing moms, we must make the choice to diligently follow the Lord, grounding ourselves in faith and hope. In doing so, not only will our relationship with Him strengthen, but we will also lay a solid foundation for our families.

Seek Him through the chaos of toddler meltdowns or the challenges of teenager tantrums. In those moments of struggle, let your faith be your anchor, knowing that He is always with you, guiding you through every trial and triumph. Embrace the journey, recognizing that each challenge is an opportunity for growth and deeper connection with Him. As you lean on His strength, you will discover a well of wisdom and resilience that equips you to navigate this beautiful yet demanding path of motherhood. Trust that your commitment to seeking Him will enrich your own spirit and serve as a powerful example for your children, showing them the importance of faith in every season of life.

There is nothing I desire more than to see you thrive as a single momma—spiritually, emotionally, physically, financially, and in every other way. Remember all that He has already done for you and your children. Reflect on those past blessings and trust that He will continue to provide for you now and in the future.

You got this.

You *are* doing this.

Seek Him in the morning.

Seek Him at night.

Seek Him in every moment in between.

Strength and honor are her clothing; she shall rejoice in time to come.

PROVERBS 31:25

About the Author

Melissa Brown is the founder and executive director of Acacia of Hope International, an organization that empowers the people of Africa spiritually, educationally, and economically. Her ministry has changed and saved thousands of lives through child sponsorship, ministry programing, church building, and more since 2012.

Melissa also has a passion for supporting and encouraging single mothers in Africa and America through ministry and her online platform, Strong Single Momma. Beyond her work as a missionary and advocate, Melissa enjoys ten mile hikes with worship music blaring and an ice-cold Dr. Pepper. She lives with her daughter in Wapakoneta, hometown of Neil Armstrong, and her pet bird Skye.

Future Reads

How do you climb from a place of immense inadequacy to a place of peace, despite your unexpected circumstance of single motherhood? *Unwavering Peace* will help you discover profound peace and rest in your single motherhood with our limitless Jesus.

You can find this book, along with other faith-based resources on Amazon and other online book stores.

Notes

1. Guzik, D. "Study Guide for Psalm 90 by David Guzik." Blue Letter Bible. Last Modified 6/2022. https://www.blueletterbible.org/comm/guzik_david/study-guide/psalm/psalm-90.cfm

2. Spurgeon, C. "Psalm 119 Verses 145-152 by C. H. Spurgeon." Blue Letter Bible. Last Modified 5 Dec 2016. https://www.blueletterbible.org/Comm/spurgeon_charles/tod/ps119_145-152.cfm

3. Guzik, D. "Study Guide for Proverbs 24 by David Guzik." Blue Letter Bible. Last Modified 6/2022. https://www.blueletterbible.org/comm/guzik_david/study-guide/proverbs/proverbs-24.cfm

4. Guzik, D. "Study Guide for Proverbs 16 by David Guzik." Blue Letter Bible. Last Modified 6/2022. https://www.blueletterbible.org/comm/guzik_david/study-guide/proverbs/proverbs-16.cfm

5. Guzik, D. "Study Guide for Psalm 128 by David Guzik." Blue Letter Bible. Last Modified 6/2022. https://www.blueletterbible.org/comm/guzik_david/study-guide/psalm/psalm-128.cfm

6. MacLaren, A. "Psalm 118 by Alexander MacLaren." Blue Letter Bible. Last Modified 15 April 2022. https://www.blueletterbible.org/comm/maclaren_alexander/the-expositors-bible/psalms-volume-three/psalm-one-hundred-eighteen.cfm

7. Spurgeon, C. "Psalm 127 by C. H. Spurgeon." Blue Letter Bible. Last Modified 5 Dec 2016. https://www.blueletterbible.org/Comm/spurgeon_charles/tod/ps127.cfm

8. Guzik, D. "Study Guide for Proverbs 21 by David Guzik." Blue Letter Bible. Last Modified 6/2022. https://www.blueletterbible.org/comm/guzik_david/study-guide/proverbs/proverbs-21.cfm

9. Guzik, D. "Study Guide for Isaiah 54 by David Guzik." Blue Letter Bible. Last Modified 6/2022. https://www.blueletterbible.org/comm/guzik_david/study-guide/isaiah/isaiah-54.cfm

10. Guzik, D. "Study Guide for Proverbs 27 by David Guzik." Blue Letter Bible. Last Modified 6/2022. https://www.blueletterbible.org/comm/guzik_david/study-guide/proverbs/proverbs-27.cfm